MEDICAL
ETHICS

THE ENCYCLOPEDIA OF
H E A L T H

MEDICAL ISSUES

Dale C. Garell, M.D. · General Editor

MEDICAL
ETHICS

Jeffrey Finn and
Eliot L. Marshall

Introduction by C. Everett Koop, M.D., Sc.D.
former Surgeon General, U.S. Public Health Service

CHELSEA HOUSE PUBLISHERS
New York · Philadelphia

The goal of the ENCYCLOPEDIA OF HEALTH *is to provide general information in the ever-changing areas of physiology, psychology, and related medical issues. The titles in this series are not intended to take the place of the professional advice of a physician or other health-care professional.*

Chelsea House Publishers
EDITOR-IN-CHIEF Nancy Toff
EXECUTIVE EDITOR Remmel T. Nunn
MANAGING EDITOR Karyn Gullen Browne
COPY CHIEF Juliann Barbato
PICTURE EDITOR   Adrian G. Allen
ART DIRECTOR   Maria Epes
MANUFACTURING MANAGER Gerald Levine

The Encyclopedia of Health
SENIOR EDITOR Paula Edelson

Staff for MEDICAL ETHICS
ASSISTANT EDITOR Nicole Bowen
DEPUTY COPY CHIEF Mark Rifkin
COPY EDITOR Philip Koslow
EDITORIAL ASSISTANT Leigh Hope Wood
PICTURE RESEARCHER Georganne Backman
ASSISTANT ART DIRECTOR Loraine Machlin
SENIOR DESIGNER Marjorie Zaum
DESIGN ASSISTANT Debora Smith
PRODUCTION MANAGER Joseph Romano
PRODUCTION COORDINATOR Marie Claire Cebrián

First Printing

1 3 5 7 9 8 6 4 2

Library of Congress Cataloging-in-Publication Data

Marshall, Eliot,
   Medical ethics/Eliot Marshall and Jeffrey Finn.
      p.   cm.—(The Encyclopedia of health. Medical issues)
   Includes bibliographical references.
   Summary: Discusses various aspects of medical ethics, including high-tech sexual reproduction, organ transplants, and the allocation of scarce resources.
   ISBN 0-7910-0086-9
        0-7910-0523-2 (pbk.)
   1. Medical ethics—Juvenile literature.   [1. Medical ethics.]
I. Finn, Jeff.   II. Title.   III. Series.
R724.M188 1990   89-25294
174'.2—dc20   CIP

CONTENTS

PREVENTION AND EDUCATION: THE KEYS TO GOOD HEALTH

C. Everett Koop, M.D., Sc.D.
former Surgeon General,
U.S. Public Health Service

The issue of health education has received particular attention in recent years because of the presence of AIDS in the news. But our response to this particular tragedy points up a number of broader issues that doctors, public health officials, educators, and the public face. In particular, it points up the necessity for sound health education for citizens of all ages.

Over the past 25 years this country has been able to bring about dramatic declines in the death rates for heart disease, stroke, accidents, and, for people under the age of 45, cancer. Today, Americans generally eat better and take better care of themselves than ever before. Thus, with the help of modern science and technology, they have a better chance of surviving serious—even catastrophic—illnesses. That's the good news.

But, like every phonograph record, there's a flip side, and one with special significance for young adults. According to a report issued in 1979 by Dr. Julius Richmond, my predecessor as Surgeon General, Americans aged 15 to 24 had a higher death rate in 1979 than they did 20 years earlier. The causes: violent death and injury, alcohol and drug abuse, unwanted pregnancies, and sexually transmitted diseases. Adolescents are particularly vulnerable, because they are beginning to explore their own sexuality and perhaps to experiment with drugs. The need for educating young people is critical, and the price of neglect is high.

Yet even for the population as a whole, our health is still far from what it could be. Why? A 1974 Canadian government report attributed all death and disease to four broad elements: inadequacies in the health-care system, behavioral factors or unhealthy life-styles, environmental hazards, and human biological factors.

To be sure, there are diseases that are still beyond the control of even our advanced medical knowledge and techniques. And despite yearnings that are as old as the human race itself, there is no "fountain of youth" to ward off aging and death. Still, there is a solution to many of the problems that undermine sound health. In a word, that solution is prevention. Prevention, which includes health promotion and education, saves lives, improves the quality of life, and, in the long run, saves money.

In the United States, organized public health activities and preventive medicine have a long history. Important milestones include the improvement of sanitary procedures and the development of pasteurized milk in the late 19th century, and the introduction in the mid-20th century of effective vaccines against polio, measles, German measles, mumps, and other once-rampant diseases. Internationally, organized public health efforts began on a wide-scale basis with the International Sanitary Conference of 1851, to which 12 nations sent representatives. The World Health Organization, founded in 1948, continues these efforts under the aegis of the United Nations, with particular emphasis on combatting communicable diseases and the training of health-care workers.

But despite these accomplishments, much remains to be done in the field of prevention. For too long, we have had a medical care system that is science- and technology-based, focused, essentially, on illness and mortality. It is now patently obvious that both the social and the economic costs of such a system are becoming insupportable.

Implementing prevention—and its corollaries, health education and promotion—is the job of several groups of people:

First, the medical and scientific professions need to continue basic scientific research, and here we are making considerable progress. But increased concern with prevention will also have a decided impact on how primary-care doctors practice medicine. With a shift to health-based rather than morbidity-based medicine, the role of the "new physician" will include a healthy dose of patient education.

Second, practitioners of the social and behavioral sciences—psychologists, economists, city planners—along with lawyers, business leaders, and government officials—must solve the practical and ethical dilemmas confronting us: poverty, crime, civil rights, literacy, education, employment, housing, sanitation, environmental protection, health care delivery systems, and so forth. All of these issues affect public health.

Third is the public at large. We'll consider that very important group in a moment.

Fourth, and the linchpin in this effort, is the public health profession—doctors, epidemiologists, teachers—who must harness the professional expertise of the first two groups and the common sense and cooperation of the third, the public. They must define the problems statistically and qualitatively and then help us set priorities for finding the solutions.

To a very large extent, improving those statistics is the responsibility of every individual. So let's consider more specifically what the role of the individual should be and why health education is so important to that role. First, and most obviously, individuals can protect themselves from illness and injury and thus minimize their need for professional medical care. They can eat a nutritious diet, get adequate exercise, avoid tobacco, alcohol, and drugs, and take prudent steps to avoid accidents. The proverbial "apple a day keeps the doctor away" is not so far from the truth, after all.

Second, individuals should actively participate in their own medical care. They should schedule regular medical and dental checkups. Should they develop an illness or injury, they should know when to treat themselves and when to seek professional help. To gain the maximum benefit from any medical treatment that they do require, individuals must become partners in that treatment. For instance, they should understand the effects and side effects of medications. I counsel young physicians that there is no such thing as too much information when talking with patients. But the corollary is the patient must know enough about the nuts and bolts of the healing process to understand what the doctor is telling him. That is at least partially the patient's responsibility.

Education is equally necessary for us to understand the ethical and public policy issues in health care today. Sometimes individuals will encounter these issues in making decisions about their own treatment or that of family members. Other citizens may encounter them as jurors in medical malpractice cases. But we all become involved, indirectly, when we elect our public officials, from school board members to the president. Should surrogate parenting be legal? To what extent is drug testing desirable, legal, or necessary? Should there be public funding for family planning, hospitals, various types of medical research, and medical care for the indigent? How should we allocate scant technological resources, such as kidney dialysis and organ transplants? What is the proper role of government in protecting the rights of patients?

What are the broad goals of public health in the United States today? In 1980, the Public Health Service issued a report aptly entitled *Promoting Health-Preventing Disease: Objectives for the Nation.*This report expressed its goals in terms of mortality and in terms of intermediate goals in education and health improvement. It identified 15 major concerns: controlling high blood pressure; improving family planning; improving pregnancy care and infant health; increasing the rate of immunization; controlling sexually transmitted diseases; controlling the presence of toxic agents and radiation in the environment; improving occupational safety and health; preventing accidents; promoting water fluoridation and dental health; controlling infectious diseases; decreasing smoking; decreasing alcohol and drug abuse; improving nutrition; promoting physical fitness and exercise; and controlling stress and violent behavior.

For healthy adolescents and young adults (ages 15 to 24), the specific goal was a 20% reduction in deaths, with a special focus on motor vehicle injuries and alcohol and drug abuse. For adults (ages 25 to 64), the aim was 25% fewer deaths, with a concentration on heart attacks, strokes, and cancers.

Smoking is perhaps the best example of how individual behavior can have a direct impact on health. Today cigarette smoking is recognized as the most important single preventable cause of death in our society. It is responsible for more cancers and more cancer deaths than any other known agent; is a prime risk factor for heart and blood vessel disease, chronic bronchitis, and emphysema; and is a frequent cause of complications in pregnancies and of babies born prematurely, underweight, or with potentially fatal respiratory and cardiovascular problems.

Since the release of the Surgeon General's first report on smoking in 1964, the proportion of adult smokers has declined substantially, from 43% in 1965 to 30.5% in 1985. Since 1965, 37 million people have quit smoking. Although there is still much work to be done if we are to become a "smoke-free society," it is heartening to note that public health and public education efforts—such as warnings on cigarette packages and bans on broadcast advertising—have already had significant effects.

In 1835, Alexis de Tocqueville, a French visitor to America, wrote, "In America the passion for physical well-being is general." Today, as then, health and fitness are front-page items. But with the greater scientific and technological resources now available to us, we are in a far stronger position to make good health care available to everyone. And with the greater technological threats to us as we approach the 21st century, the need to do so is more urgent than ever before. Comprehensive information about basic biology, preventive medicine, medical and surgical treatments, and related ethical and public policy issues can help you arm yourself with the knowledge you need to be healthy throughout your life.

FOREWORD

Dale C. Garell, M.D.

Advances in our understanding of health and disease during the 20th century have been truly remarkable. Indeed, it could be argued that modern health care is one of the greatest accomplishments in all of human history. In the early 1900s, improvements in sanitation, water treatment, and sewage disposal reduced death rates and increased longevity. Previously untreatable illnesses can now be managed with antibiotics, immunizations, and modern surgical techniques. Discoveries in the fields of immunology, genetic diagnosis, and organ transplantation are revolutionizing the prevention and treatment of disease. Modern medicine is even making inroads against cancer and heart disease, two of the leading causes of death in the United States.

Although there is much to be proud of, medicine continues to face enormous challenges. Science has vanquished diseases such as smallpox and polio, but new killers, most notably AIDS, confront us. Moreover, we now victimize ourselves with what some have called "diseases of choice," or those brought on by drug and alcohol abuse, bad eating habits, and mismanagement of the stresses and strains of contemporary life. The very technology that is doing so much to prolong life has brought with it previously unimaginable ethical dilemmas related to issues of death and dying. The rising cost of health-care is a matter of central concern to us all. And violence in the form of automobile accidents, homicide, and suicide remain the major killers of young adults.

In the past, most people were content to leave health care and medical treatment in the hands of professionals. But since the 1960s, the consumer of medical care—that is, the patient—has assumed an increasingly central role in the management of his or her own health. There has also been a new emphasis placed on prevention: People are recognizing that their own actions can help prevent many of the conditions that have caused death and disease in the past. This accounts for the growing commitment to good nutrition and regular exercise, for the fact that more and more people are choosing not to smoke, and for a new moderation in people's drinking habits.

People want to know more about themselves and their own health. They are curious about their body: its anatomy, physiology, and biochemistry. They want to keep up with rapidly evolving medical technologies and procedures. They are willing to educate themselves about common disorders and diseases so that they can be full partners in their own health-care.

The ENCYCLOPEDIA OF HEALTH is designed to provide the basic knowledge that readers will need if they are to take significant responsibility for their own health. It is also meant to serve as a frame of reference for further study and exploration. The ENCYCLOPEDIA is divided into five subsections: The Healthy Body; The Life Cycle; Medical Disorders & Their Treatment; Psychological Disorders & Their Treatment; and Medical Issues. For each topic covered by the ENCYCLOPEDIA, we present the essential facts about the relevant biology; the symptoms, diagnosis, and treatment of common diseases and disorders; and ways in which you can prevent or reduce the severity of health problems when that is possible. The ENCYCLOPEDIA also projects what may lie ahead in the way of future treatment or prevention strategies.

The broad range of topics and issues covered in the ENCYCLOPEDIA reflects the fact that human health encompasses physical, psychological, social, environmental, and spiritual well-being. Just as the mind and the body are inextricably linked, so, too, is the individual an integral part of the wider world that comprises his or her family, society, and environment. To discuss health in its broadest aspect it is necessary to explore the many ways in which it is connected to such fields as law, social science, public policy, economics, and even religion. And so, the ENCYCLOPEDIA is meant to be a bridge between science, medical technology, the world at large, and you. I hope that it will inspire you to pursue in greater depth particular areas of interest, and that you will take advantage of the suggestions for further reading and the lists of resources and organizations that can provide additional information.

AUTHORS'
PREFACE

Hippocrates, Galen, and Avicenna

While playing on the frozen surface of the Red River in Fargo, North Dakota, in 1987, 11-year-old Alvaro Garza, Jr., fell through the ice and lay under the bone-chilling water for 45 minutes. Rescue workers finally pulled Garza from the water, and 15 minutes later doctors at St. Luke's Hospital-MeritCare in Fargo split open the boy's chest, hooked up a heart-lung machine to warm his blood, and attached ventilators to help him breathe.

Three days later, Garza, who entered the hospital showing no signs of life, asked for a hamburger and soda.

Advanced medical technology had saved another life but at what price? According to one estimate, Alvaro Garza's rescue cost more than $100,000. That money could provide 20 pregnant low-income women with prenatal treatment that they would not otherwise have, helping to ensure the safe delivery and healthy infancy of 20 new babies. On what basis should a society decide whether to spend $100,000 to save the life of 1 child or use the money to help 20 needy mothers safely give birth to their children? Should anyone have the power to make that type of choice? How should one weigh the value of heroic rescue efforts against less dramatic but perhaps equally important ventures aimed at preventing disease and promoting health?

Such questions are no longer theoretical. Many state lawmakers already face them when they decide which surgical procedures and medical services the state's health-insurance program for low-income residents will cover. The next generation of Americans can expect to face tougher, even more troubling choices

Four-year-old Donnie Wartenberg was born with a dysfunctioning lung that had to be removed and has spent most of his life in a hospital. Science can now keep such children alive, but the cost of their care is high.

about medical care. They will have to help decide what type of care should be available, who should be entitled to it, and how much they should receive.

THE GROWING DEBATE

For many years, people in the United States and most other developed countries have expected doctors to do everything in their power to save lives. Advances in medical technologies and in the development of preventive vaccines and disease-arresting drugs have caused those expectations to soar. Logically, these breakthroughs should increase both the quality of medical care and the number of people who have access to it. But in recent years, the focus of concern in medical care has changed. The central question is no longer whether the nation has the technical knowledge to save and prolong a patient's life but rather who should receive it. To put it simply: Just because the use of medical technology can prolong a life does not mean that in every case it should be used to do so. And just because certain medical procedures are available does not mean in practice that every person who would benefit will be able to gain access to them or be able to pay for them.

Confronted with rising medical costs and sometimes limited financial and medical resources, medical professionals and ethicists are asking: When should any given course of treatment end? In the case of limited medical resources such as human organs for transplantation, on what basis should these medical resources be allocated? Who should be treated first, and who last? As medicine advances, health professionals ask with growing urgency: What is best for the patient? What is best for society? And who is to make the decisions?

WHAT IS BIOMEDICAL ETHICS?

The American Hospital Association defines *biomedical ethics* as "the study of rational processes for determining the most morally desirable course of action in the face of conflicting value choices associated with the practice of medicine." In other words, it is the field of study that considers how the best choice can be made in medical situations in which there are multiple desires that cannot all be satisfied. Conflict is always present in such choices, and that is why they are so hard to make. There are almost never any black-and-white answers. What is morally desirable to scientists or physicians, for example, may run counter to a patient's religious or moral beliefs. The challenge is to strike and maintain a delicate balance between an individual's rights and society's needs.

Allocating Scarce Resources

Much of the biomedical debate arises from a need to get the maximum benefit out of limited financial and medical resources. The debate has intensified lately as federal, state, and local governments face budget deficits and find they must cut spending or raise taxes; it has also intensified as the number of people needing to be treated for illnesses requiring enormously expensive care grows. A prime example of one such disease is *acquired immune deficiency syndrome* (AIDS)—a disease caused by a virus that destroys the immune system, leaving the victim susceptible to cancers and other fatal illnesses. Tough decisions have to be made as to which scientific research projects to fund; which medical procedures to pay for; and which patients to treat.

People in the United States now spend more than 11% of the *gross national product* (GNP)—the total value of the goods and services produced by a nation's residents—on health care every year. That figure is expected to jump to almost 15% by the beginning of the 21st century, according to the latest Department of Health and Human Services (HHS) estimates.

Although the United States—government and citizens combined—spends a greater percentage of its GNP on health care than does any other industrialized country in the world, some leading health-care officials think it is not enough. If the government is going to spend more, avoid significant tax increases, and not begin a program of directly allocating health care itself, other tax-supported programs will have to be given less. That could mean cuts in defense, space exploration, or education. As health costs rise, people with private health insurance may have to pay more for their coverage as well.

President Lyndon B. Johnson flips the pages of the 1965 Medicare bill he has just signed. Former president Harry Truman (right) originally proposed the bill two decades earlier.

THE SOCIAL SAFETY NET

Many health-policy experts claim that the country has no choice but to spend more to ensure that all Americans have at least some health insurance. In 1965, the nation took what seemed to be a major step in ensuring such insurance when President Lyndon Johnson signed into law legislation establishing the Medicare and Medicaid programs. These programs have been modified and expanded since their inception. Medicare is for those 65 and older, disabled people who have been entitled to Social Security disability benefits for a minimum of 24 consecutive months, and those who need kidney dialysis. It is administered by the federal government under the Health Care Financing Administration (HCFA), part of HHS, and is financed in part by Social Security payroll taxes. Medicare provides basic hospital insurance and voluntary medical insurance, which requires a monthly premium. Medicaid, which is administered by the individual states and financed jointly by the local, state, and federal governments, provides medical insurance to those with low incomes. The income requirements and benefits vary from state to state.

The introduction of these programs in the 1960s was an enormous step in helping those who lack private medical insurance to receive care. However, the promises of Medicare and Medicaid have fallen short. As modern science and changes in eating habits and living conditions keep people alive longer, an increasing number of elderly people need long-term care. This care may cover a broad range, extending from intensive nursing-home care to part-time home care to occasional care in specially designed retirement communities. And many elderly people find the only way they can "afford" the $26,000 average annual cost of skilled nursing-home care, for example, is to spend everything they own until they have nothing left and are literally impoverished. Only at that point will Medicaid take over.

Proponents of reforming the current U.S. health-care system also point out that currently 1 in 6 Americans—almost 37 million people—has no health insurance. This number is growing, in part because the rising cost of insurance has forced many small businesses to stop providing health insurance as an employment benefit. Also, because each state is now spending an increased portion of Medicaid funds on the low-income elderly, there is less for other low-income groups. Thus the main reason the number of uninsured poor has increased so dramatically is that the states have changed their eligibility requirements for Medicaid.

The cost for care provided to those lacking insurance, moreover, is passed on to those who have private insurance policies through higher health-insurance premiums; to federal, state, and local governments; and to hospitals that treat the *medically indigent*, those without insurance or money to cover the cost of their care. A crisis may be in the offing. Those who pay for private health insurance are balking at subsidizing such "free" care, and the governments and hospitals are reaching the point at which they are no longer able to afford providing such care without jeopardizing access to high-quality health care for the patients who fully pay their costs—the vast majority of Americans.

Many health-policy analysts urge federal, state, and local governments to redirect funds toward health-promotion and disease-prevention programs. They point out that 19 countries had lower infant mortality rates than the United States did in 1985. The rationale behind their argument sounds simple enough: Keep people fit now so they do not have to use more costly medical services later. For example, research shows that for every dollar the country spends on preventive prenatal care, it will save about three dollars in postnatal expenses.

THE CHALLENGE OF NEW TECHNOLOGY

One reason technology has raised an ethical challenge is that it has "popularized" medicines and techniques that were once available only in specialized treatment centers. Twenty years ago, for example, most surgical procedures were performed in hospitals where patients were admitted as live-in guests and often stayed several days, even for relatively minor operations. Today, surgeons perform hundreds of those same services—including cataract surgery—in their offices, hospital outpatient clinics (which treat patients without admitting them overnight), or freestanding

Because many low-income pregnant women do not receive enough prenatal care, their babies often have low birth weights and may suffer various physical and developmental problems.

surgical centers (units set up to do surgery but not connected to hospitals). Patients walk in for the operation and walk out the same day to recover at home. This has greatly reduced the potential demand for hospital beds, but at the same time, as these procedures have become available to more citizens, the demand for them has increased. Therefore, new technology making it easier to perform surgery has not meant that the total national expenditure on surgery has decreased. Just the opposite has happened: It has grown tremendously.

Another reason for this increased expenditure is the development of high-tech procedures and treatments, which are often very costly. Many health policymakers ask whether the government should consider placing limits on the availability of certain types of surgery. At what point should the cost of a medical service be weighed against the social benefit of that procedure? It is not just the financial problems created by new medical technology that are worrisome. The dizzying pace of innovation raises fundamental questions about the meaning of life: Where must one draw the line to preserve dignity and respect for the individual? Medical advances on a host of scientific fronts— including organ transplantation, fetal surgery, and genetic engineering—keep people alive longer but also fuel this debate. For example, in the quest to save and extend life, doctors have attempted to keep a newborn alive by implanting organs taken from a baboon. Some victims of Parkinson's disease have been subjects of experimental brain implants using tissue from aborted fetuses. Are there limits to what medical science and research should do?

THE BRITISH EXAMPLE

British doctors, who provide care for every British citizen through the National Health Service, have found it necessary to employ an allocation scheme for certain costly procedures and medical devices. For example, many elderly people who need hip replacements find themselves on long waiting lists for this *optional procedure* (treatment for a non-life-threatening condition). But younger people who need the same procedure are placed ahead of the elderly on waiting lists because they are considered

Because more people than ever before are living to old age, quality of life for the elderly is becoming an increasingly pertinent issue.

"more productive" members of society. Is this just? Is it right to make age the key consideration? Should there be other measures of need? If so, what are they? These questions stir strong emotions on both sides of the debate over the age-based rationing of health care. Meanwhile, these issues are irrelevant for those in Britain who are fortunate enough to be able to afford comprehensive private health insurance. These people are able to pay for the treatment they want.

QUALITY OF LIFE

The aging of America's population has brought another ethical question to the fore; this has to do with the quality of life. Although people may live longer now, partly as a result of improvements in medicine, there are concerns about the kind of life they will enjoy during the additional, last years they have acquired. The longer a person lives, the greater the chances he or she has of suffering from one or more chronic health problems. People age 85 and older are 4 times more likely to be disabled by these health problems than people age 65 to 74, who in turn are much more likely to suffer disability than are those under 65. Increased levels of disability mean increased spending for health-care services, many of which are funded through public programs.

These statistics indicate that society should confront with greater frequency the difficult question of whether to "pull the plug" on heroic medical treatment for people who can hope for only modest improvements in the quality of their life. The same problem confronts the families of patients who suffer chronic degenerative diseases, such as AIDS and some forms of cancer, for which there are no present cures. In these cases, the question is: Should the expensive "band-aid" measures (treatments that can only temporarily alleviate symptoms) that technology makes available be used, or should the medical community wait until science comes up with true cures for the diseases in question before making treatment widely available?

CONFRONTING ETHICS DAILY

Discussions of biomedical ethics can easily fall into the realm of theory. Although it is important for society to address questions from a broad perspective, answering these questions for society as a whole, it is also important to understand that doctors and other health-care professionals make life-and-death decisions every hour of every day in hospitals, nursing homes, and hospices about the limits and quality of care patients receive.

As the gatekeepers to medical care in this country, physicians are at the heart of ethical decisions concerning how much care should be given and whether and when it should be terminated. Ideally, those decisions take into account the needs and wishes of patients and families as well as those of large institutions. Hospitals often bring together patients, families, physicians, and hospital staff to discuss such volatile issues as *do-not-resuscitate (DNR) orders* (which give guidelines for when certain treatments should cease, allowing death to take its natural course), *euthanasia* (the assisted or unassisted suicide of a terminally or chronically ill person), patients' rights to refuse treatment, and rationing of health-care services. Hospitals often have standing committees to promote ongoing educational programs for medical professionals about ethical issues. These committees also serve as a source of information and advice for those who must routinely make ethical decisions affecting life and death. In addition to hospital committees, there are organizations set up to educate health professionals about various ethical issues. One such organization is the Society for Health and Human Values, which conducts programs at national meetings and acts as a resource for educational institutions.

For example, hospital committees and these professional organizations are being called on to advise medical staff about responsibilities concerning AIDS. Fear of AIDS has sparked debate over patients' rights versus the public's right to be protected. Should all Americans be tested for the deadly virus even though the risk of contracting the disease is low for most of the population? On what basis, if any, should physicians and other health-care workers be excused from treating patients with AIDS? And should patients be told they are being cared for by someone with AIDS? The ethics of AIDS extends beyond hospitals, however; state and federal lawmakers have to decide how much to spend for treatment and for research and education efforts to stop the spread of the disease. Those decisions are important not only because of the seriousness of the AIDS crisis but also because spending in one area usually means limiting research and treatment in other areas of medicine.

AIDS has brought to the fore other questions of ethics relating to medical personnel. An October 1989 *New York Times* editorial expressed the opinion that ethics and responsibilities should be presented to students *before* they choose to enter medical school. It even suggests they be asked to take the Hippocratic oath at the beginning of medical school to encourage them to think about demands placed on doctors. The author, Lawrence K. Altman, M.D., feels that some doctors today have forgotten that medicine is historically a dangerous field—less than a century ago health-care workers risked their life to treat those with polio, syphilis, tuberculosis, and other communicable diseases.

The aim of this book is to present some of the major ethical problems that have come to the forefront of medicine in recent years. These problems are likely to become even more complicated in the 1990s as technology becomes more sophisticated and public funds become more tightly controlled.

●   ●   ●   ●

CHAPTER 1

AN EVOLVING ETHIC OF PRACTICE

Hippocrates

I will prescribe regimen for the good of my patients according to my ability and judgment and never do harm to anyone." This is part of a code of medical ethics that has existed for thousands of years. Doctors today still pledge to uphold the Hippocratic oath, named after Hippocrates (ca. 460–ca. 377 B.C.), the ancient Greek physician credited with separating medicine from religion and magic. Although his writings formed the early basis on which medical ethics were to be built, it is interesting that a similar idea was expressed almost a thousand years earlier in the oath taken by physicians of the Hindu religion: "Do the sick no harm."

This principle has been the bedrock of ethical conduct on which physicians and other health-care professionals have founded their practice of medicine. But under increasing economic and social pressures, that directive has become mired in controversy. This debate, in part, has led to the emergence of professional medical ethicists. Most medical ethicists hold a Ph.D. in philosophy, often in bio-philosophy, and sometimes in religious studies.

Medical science has enabled providers of health care to keep patients alive longer, often through seemingly miraculous procedures that were inconceivable only a few years earlier. Advances in medical technologies and medical procedures tempt physicians to push the limits of what they try to do for patients in the pursuit of doing no harm. But health-care professionals have come to realize that abiding by that traditional charge also means facing tougher decisions about when to pull back from aggressive treatment that may prolong life but not enhance its quality. Sometimes doing less, not more, they argue, is in the best interest of the patient.

Thus, the oath that today's physicians swear to uphold is more complex than Hippocrates' oath, but the essence of the message remains focused on taking all necessary steps to meet the patient's needs. Ironically, today's response to Hippocrates' call for physicians to help often means honoring a patient's request to discontinue use of life-support equipment. The limits of what it means to abide by the Hippocratic oath also have been tested through time by physicians and medical researchers seeking to advance the science of medicine. Medical research seems particularly vulnerable to such questions. For example, at what point do the rights of an individual participating in an experiment become less important than the larger societal good that could be derived from the medical experiment?

UNETHICAL EXPERIMENTS

Unfortunately, in pursuit of medical knowledge, some scientists in the 20th century have set grim precedents for the kind of research behavior that should not be tolerated. Their record demonstrates why it is important to adhere to the ethical principles of medical practice and respect the rights of the individual.

In 1932, for example, the U.S. Public Health Service initiated a study to examine the effects of untreated syphilis (a serious chronic sexually transmitted disease) on human subjects. The 600 participants in what came to be known as the Tuskegee Study were all low-income blacks—399 of whom had contracted syphilis and 201 without it who were to act as a control group, or comparison group. Despite claims that all the subjects (many of whom were illiterate) were volunteers who had given consent, it seems clear that the men who participated had little clear understanding of the risks they were taking or of the alternative of seeking treatment. The meager incentives offered—free medical checkups, which some took to be treatments for their condition, hot meals on checkup days, and a promise of free burial—were enough to induce these men to agree to participate in the study.

The subjects in this study were monitored for 40 years but were not treated for syphilis. When the study began in 1932,

Doctors examining a subject of the Tuskegee Study in the 1930s. The people who participated in the study were mainly poor and illiterate black men who had little understanding of the risks they were taking or of treatment alternatives.

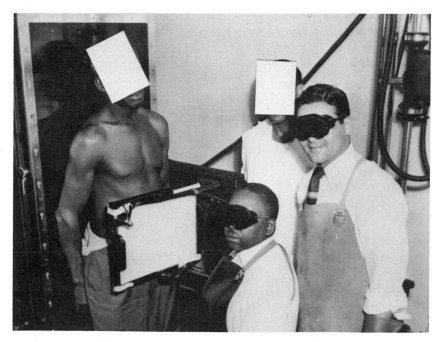

there was not yet an effective treatment, but by the 1940s the antibiotic penicillin was available. By 1969, at least 28 of the men had died of syphilis, more than 150 had died from other causes, and the Public Health Service had performed autopsies on all of the dead to study the effects of untreated syphilis. When details of the experiment came to light in 1972, the nation was stunned. The study ended only after it was publicly disclosed. The subjects still alive and the families of those who had died did pursue a lawsuit, but before it came to trial they accepted the government's offer to make a cash settlement, provide health care, and pay funeral costs. The surviving volunteers and heirs of the deceased received payments ranging from $5,000 to $37,500.

Another deplorable case involved the egregious experiments Nazi physicians carried out during World War II. The subjects were not unwitting volunteers but prisoners in concentration camps who were forced to participate. In one experiment, almost 300 prisoners in the Dachau concentration camp were stripped naked and immersed in vats of near-freezing water. A surgeon for the Luftwaffe, the German air force, wanted to understand the effects of hypothermia (subnormal body temperature) on pilots who might be shot down over water during combat. The experiments were conducted under strict conditions, and records were carefully maintained; but, as the doctor tried various techniques of raising the body temperature, at least 80 of the prisoners died. The work violated innumerable tenets of ethical behavior.

Ironically, more than two dozen scientific research papers on hypothermia have drawn on findings from the Dachau experiments. Two recent examples of these are studies done in 1984 by John Hayward at the University of Victoria, British Columbia, and in 1988 by the physiology department at the University of Minnesota. In addition, several companies petitioned two U.S. government agencies in 1988 for approval of certain drugs and medical technologies on the basis of the data gathered by Nazi scientists. After review by internal ethics panels at each agency, the requests were turned down—primarily because of the way in which the information was gathered. Ethics panel members said they feared acceptance of the information might lead other medical researchers, who are under tremendous economic pressure to produce scientific breakthroughs, to seek shortcuts and thus engage in ethically unacceptable practices.

A few leading medical ethicists, including Arthur L. Caplan, director of the Center for Biomedical Ethics at the University of Minnesota, however, have argued that even if the findings from the Dachau experiments and other Nazi atrocities were obtained through evil means, it is acceptable to use this information to save lives. The debate is unlikely to subside.

THE ROLE OF THE ETHICIST

Although no nation can oversee the activities of all its physicians and medical researchers, awareness of the ethical implications in medicine broadened enormously during the 1970s and 1980s. Medical ethicists founded the Hastings Center in Hastings-on-Hudson, in 1969, and the Kennedy Institute of Ethics at Georgetown University in Washington, D.C., in 1971. These organizations, in turn, have spawned an expanding number of similar institutions across the country. Many university medical centers, which often treat the most severely ill patients, now have medical ethicists on staff to assist staff and patients.

The emerging role of the ethicist as an active participant in health-care delivery is a relatively new phenomenon. The need reflects the diversity of new choices available to medical personnel and the changing relationship between patient and doctor as well as the increasingly complex legal implications of medical decisions.

As science has created new technologies and drugs to treat patients, expectations about what medicine can and should do for patients has changed. Organ transplants, *in vitro fertilization* (IVF)—test-tube fertilization of an egg—kidney dialysis, and heart pacemakers with minicomputers implanted in the chest of heart attack patients are among the host of advances that have helped fuel expectations that medical science can perform miracles.

For example, a normal pregnancy lasts about 40 weeks, and the full-term baby averages more than 6 pounds. But advances in medical science have enabled highly skilled physicians at the best-equipped hospitals to keep 28-week-old babies alive in

Scientific advances have enabled doctors to keep alive babies born as much as 12 weeks prematurely. The cost for such care, however, can be staggering.

roughly 90% to 95% of the cases. Such an infant may weigh slightly more than two pounds, with hands the size of quarters and veins as thin as a hair.

Armed with state-of-the-art tools, doctors often expect perfection of themselves, and they are sometimes reluctant to discuss what they consider to be failures in treating patients. Patients, often mystified and awed by the array of devices and medicines available to their physicians, can also fall prey to those same illusions of perfection.

While advances in medicine have heightened expectations about what medicine can and should do, they also have created uneasiness among many elderly patients. Procedures such as cataract surgery once required that patients be hospitalized for several days. After recent advances, however, virtually all such operations are now done on an outpatient basis, meaning that the individual goes home the same day of the operation. Ironically, some elderly patients whose friends were hospitalized for a similar operation only a few years earlier worry that they are being denied adequate treatment when they find themselves cared for in a new way using more up-to-date technologies.

THE CHANGING PATIENT-PHYSICIAN
RELATIONSHIP

Clearly, changes in the delivery of health-care services and the payment for those services are having a profound effect on the patient-physician relationship. In addition, as medicine has become more technologically advanced, it has seen a dramatic increase in the number of medical specialists.

In the relatively recent past, a family practitioner would refer his or her patients to a specialist only on the rarest of occasions. But the family doctor of the 1980s routinely refers patients to specialists to perform a variety of high-tech services, such as extracorporeal shock wave lithotripsy or nuclear magnetic resonance imaging, procedures with almost mind-numbing names for the average patient. Although the techniques and the precision of diagnoses may have improved greatly over those of the past, the change to greater emphasis on medical specialists also means that a greater number of people are involved in medical decision making.

Many physicians and medical ethicists worry that these changes may be diminishing the amount of trust that has traditionally existed between patients and physicians. That trust is essential in forging substantive patient-physician relationships and enabling medical personnel to understand the wishes of patients if they face life-threatening or life-sustaining treatment decisions.

The Ethics of AIDS

The current AIDS epidemic has raised new and often painful ethical dilemmas. Questions about the degree to which health-care personnel should honor the confidentiality of patient records threaten to undermine patient-physician relationships.

Consider, for example, a case before the district court in Johnson County, Kansas. A married man, the father of two children, went to his doctor because he feared that he might have contracted the *human immunodeficiency virus* (HIV)—the virus that causes AIDS—through his use of an infected hypodermic needle. Although the doctor had warned the man that he was at risk of getting AIDS if he used drugs intravenously, the man ignored the advice. The case was further complicated because the man's wife did not know her husband used drugs.

When the man's blood tests confirmed that he did indeed have AIDS, the doctor urged him to tell his wife about his addiction to drugs and his test results. He refused, arguing that his wife and children would abandon him.

In such cases, does the physician have a stronger responsibility to honor the wishes of his patient or to inform the family of the father's potentially fatal disease, a disease he could pass on to his wife through sexual contact? In what is believed to be the first such decision nationwide, the Kansas court ruled in late 1988 that the man's health clinic did not have the legal right to tell his wife the results of her husband's AIDS-virus test results, even though he tested positive. The judge based this decision on the principle of physician-patient confidentiality, which the judge felt held more weight than did the woman's right to know.

Medical-Care Delivery Systems

Another factor that could undermine the physician-patient relationship is the proliferation of new types of medical-care delivery systems. Patients can choose from what seems an endless alphabet soup of health-care plans: HMOs (health maintenance organizations), IPAs (independent practice associations), PPOs (preferred provider organizations), or CMPs (competitive medical plans).

In essence, these plans represent a new way to manage the delivery and cost of medical care by bringing together teams of health-care professionals. In such so-called managed-care plans, the group practice receives a fixed monthly fee per patient from an employer or insurance company. Patients are usually free to go to the medical practice as often as they wish, paying only a small fee for each appointment. Although patients may request to see a particular physician, chances are good that they will have to see whoever is available.

In managed-care plans, the loss of trust in physician-patient relationships may go further; ethical problems may arise because these plans have a financial incentive to give the least care possible. The less care they provide, the lower their costs, and the more money they make on the fixed monthly per-patient payment.

Arnold S. Relman, M.D., editor in chief of the *New England Journal of Medicine*, warned in a September 1988 editorial that the drive to control costs and to make medicine into a competitive, commercial enterprise threatened to "reduce physicians to vendors." He concluded: "No physician should enter into any arrangement offering rewards for withholding services or for increasing the use of services."

The practice of medicine is changing. Not long ago, the vast majority of physicians in the United States were in independent practices. Now, with a glut of practitioners in many specialty areas and the rising cost of malpractice insurance in certain fields, more physicians, especially those just out of medical school, are taking salaried positions with HMOs and hospitals.

In 1988, New York governor Mario Cuomo (seated) signed into law a bill guaranteeing confidentiality to AIDS patients.

The change does not necessarily endanger quality of care, but it does raise ethical concerns if the institution that hires the physician is driven primarily by a profit motive. In such cases, physicians may feel strong economic pressures that can influence their medical decision making. Other forces may create those pressures as well. Public and private institutions that pay health-care bills are scrutinizing medical decisions more diligently than ever. Treatments that these establishments deem unnecessary or inappropriate are not paid for, leaving physicians and patients to bear the brunt of rapidly escalating costs. Health insurers are also requiring patients to obtain second opinions from medical professionals other than their own doctor before undergoing certain surgical procedures. Many physicians adamantly object to what they see as the intrusion of cost concerns and other demands into the practice of medicine. One physician expressed his frustration about the changing environment by submitting what he called "A Contemporary Physician's Oath" for publication in the *New England Journal of Medicine*.

In part, the oath read: "I will reveal to any of my offspring who aspire to join our profession the terrible pressures of the practice of medicine today, including professional liability, restricted freedom in the methods of treating illness and the use of hospitals and the prescribing of medicines, and the hostile relationship with patients that has developed because of the insidious rationing of health care (Medicare), regulations of health maintenance organizations (HMOs), and so on."

The reverse of this situation can also be a problem. There are unethical doctors in private practice, which operates on a fee-for-service basis, who will recommend and perform unnecessary treatments for monetary gain.

Without doubt, there are new pressures that have come to bear on patient-physician relationships, changes that raise ethical questions about whether the best of medical care is being given and should be given to all patients.

Patient Autonomy

Still another factor changing the traditional relationship between patients and physicians in the delivery of medical care is that patients are becoming more autonomous. Advances in some medical technologies, such as kidney dialysis, now enable many individuals to receive care at home, whereas only years earlier they routinely might have gone for service to their physicians' offices or to hospitals. Although such treatments are conducted in close consultation with physicians, patients in many instances are no longer reliant on physicians to deliver that care personally. With the increased awareness in health and fitness, many people are more informed and therefore more critical health-care consumers. In recent years, the number of books on medicine for the average reader has greatly increased, as have the number of television shows and magazine articles. Many local newspapers have a special health column. While being knowledgeable is good, this may also strain patient-physician relationships.

Medical advancements, too, could further strain the patient-physician relationship in the future. Developments include devices that patients could use at home and that provide easy, effective, nearly continuous monitoring of physical conditions, moods, or mental states. Such devices would allow people themselves to define health and illness, relying less on doctors for diagnosis. Some futurists also envision individuals using a wristwatch-type device that would perform many of the diagnostic functions now performed by physicians and hospitals. Such a tool could, for example, monitor blood pressure and heart rate and feed the data into a home computer programmed to detect changes that require medical attention.

Malpractice Lawsuits

One reflection of the changing relationship between physicians and patients is the burgeoning number of medical malpractice lawsuits filed against medical personnel in the 1970s and 1980s. Multimillion-dollar jury awards have become common. The deluge of such high-priced awards has had a marked impact on the delivery of medicine.

Arthur L. Caplan, a medical ethicist, remarked at a 1987 Washington, D.C., conference of state Medicaid directors, "Patients don't tell doctors the truth or don't follow instructions about medication; they keep secrets because of a perceived lack of confidentiality in their relationship with their doctor." And, as a result of the breakdown in trust, he continued, patients are quick to sue.

As jury awards have grown larger, medical malpractice insurance premiums have become extremely expensive, prohibitively so for many specialties, such as obstetrics, in certain parts of the country. Fear of lawsuits has also prompted physicians to practice what is commonly described as *defensive medicine*—care or tests that are, by and large, unnecessary. In the mid-1980s, the American Medical Association estimated that up to 30% of medical costs were for defensive medicine.

Two recent reports dramatically underscore the depth of the problem.

- In September 1987, the *Journal of the American Medical Association* published a study that concluded that of the 100,000 elective coronary bypass operations performed annually in the United States, as many as half may be unneeded.

- In January 1988, the *New England Journal of Medicine* published the findings of researchers in Pennsylvania who studied medical records of 382 patients receiving heart pacemakers in 1983. In more than one-third of the cases, the need for implantation of the device was "unclear," and in another one-fifth of the cases, the device was clearly *not* needed. More than 120,000 pacemakers are implanted annually in the United States, at a total cost of almost $2 billion. If the findings from the Pennsylvania study are applied nationwide, more than half the pacemaker implants and more than $1 billion in such expenditures are unnecessary.

Although doctors swear to do no harm, is giving too much care unethical? Although such care may be medically unnecessary, it is prudent behavior on the part of the physician who fears being sued for not doing everything possible to cure the patient. Thus physicians may almost feel obliged to err on the side of overtreatment. Patient advocates, however, note that given the increasing efforts the medical community has made to cut costs, ensuring that patients receive good medical care is increasingly important to monitor. Patients' ability to file medical malpractice

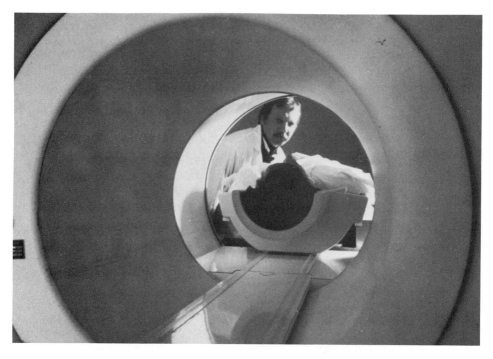

As medical technology becomes increasingly complex and patients deal more frequently with specialists as opposed to a general practitioner or family doctor, the relationship between patient and doctor changes.

suits acts as a check against cutting corners in the medical system, they argue.

Although its effects on the quality of patient care are unclear, the malpractice crisis has had a tangible effect on patient access to health-care services. The increases in insurance premiums have led some obstetricians and gynecologists to stop caring for pregnant women and delivering babies, choosing instead to perform only routine gynecological care. Some hospitals have shut down emergency-room services.

The question arises, however, as to whether the United States can afford to let multimillion-dollar malpractice awards for a few hinder access to medical care for tens of thousands of others. Do federal and state governments have an ethical responsibility to step in and set limits on the monetary damages a person is entitled to for "pain and suffering"? In a sense, such judgments themselves lead to pain and suffering for those who have no access to care.

Beginning in the mid-1980s, state governments began to answer that question. An increasing number of state lawmakers voted to limit the size of malpractice settlements for pain and suffering in an effort to keep doctors providing needed services for the society at large. Despite such actions, physicians and other providers of health care will continue to face medical dilemmas that not only put them at risk for malpractice charges but also raise complex biomedical questions.

The most prominent dilemmas usually occur in situations at the beginning of life or at the end of it—with the newborn and the elderly. But the ethical basis of medical practice defies neat categorization by time or place. Ideally, it seeks to provide the greatest good for the largest number of patients, at all times.

What appears certain is that difficult decisions will be confronted with increasing regularity as patient-physician relationships continue to be changed by new medical technologies, evolving practice patterns, increasing cost pressures, and a heightened awareness of the rights of patients.

●　　　　●　　　　●　　　　●

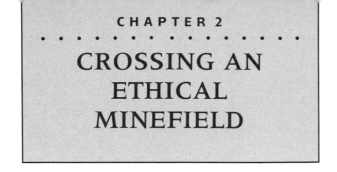

CHAPTER 2

· · · · · · · · · · · · · · ·

CROSSING AN
ETHICAL
MINEFIELD

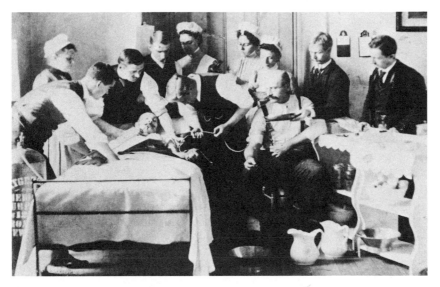

A blood transfusion in Bellevue Hospital, New York City, about 1890

D r. Elliott Osserman, a cancer researcher at Columbia-Presbyterian Medical Center in New York, has the early symptoms of Parkinson's disease. It is a slow-moving disorder of the nervous system that gradually robs the victim of all independence. Speech becomes slurred, body movement erratic, posture stooped. Many sufferers end up entirely dependent on family, friends, and nurses for the simplest functions, such as eating and washing.

Osserman drew attention when his daughter appeared on the ABC News television show "Nightline" in 1988. She was asked about an experimental therapy in which doctors implant fetal tissue in the brain of a Parkinson's victim to slow the progress of the disease. On camera, she said she would be willing to conceive a child, then abort the fetus in order to help her father. Both she and her sister offered to do this. Dr. Osserman said, "I would not accept it. Categorically, no. It would be wrong to sacrifice a new life to sustain an old one."

But not everyone with Parkinson's might object. It is almost certain that if the fetal implant technique succeeds, doctors will come under more pressure to use it. Some women may consider doing what Osserman's daughter proposed. As Ted Koppel, host of "Nightline," said, "we are entering an ethical minefield."

There are an estimated 750,000 to 1 million *spontaneous abortions* (miscarriages) and another 1.6 million *induced abortions* (those purposely brought about by various procedures) each year in the United States. This means there is enough fetal tissue to satisfy the potential demand of Parkinson's patients if the therapy proves effective. Although it is possible that the procedure may prove ineffective, the chance that it might work raises interesting questions. Is it right to treat fetal tissue like blood, semen, urine, and other tissue, all of which are used in experiments? Or should a developing embryo be given special respect? When exactly does an aborted fetus "die," and at what point should it be made available for research?

If fetal implants in the brain effectively treat Parkinson's disease, should the procedure be made widely available? Or would it be better to limit it to research? Widespread use might create the nightmare that ethicists worry about—a large trade in fetal tissue, with potential for abuse. Pressures to collect tissue in a timely fashion would increase. Having an abortion might be seen in a less negative light and might be considered a generous act—somewhat like donating blood to a blood bank. Poor women, particularly those outside the United States where controls might be looser, might be paid to provide fetal tissue. This could easily be perceived as unethical, even by those who may benefit from such an endeavor. Dr. Ossserman's daughter, reflecting on her own offer to have an abortion, agreed that there was an element of "Frankenstein" in her proposal. Should research on fetal tissue be forbidden in order to remove such pressures?

These are difficult questions to which no one has clear answers. Such issues dominate ethical discussions of fetal-tissue use, as well as debates on many new medical procedures. Medical and ethical leaders are struggling to develop guidelines that will seem fair and just to all concerned.

In 1988, for example, Robert E. Windom, M.D., then assistant secretary for health in HHS, ordered a halt to federal research on fetal tissue from induced abortions. He then set up a review committee of experts to study the issue. The preliminary conclusion, made public by the National Institutes of Health (NIH) in December 1988, was unanimous: The research should continue. But that recommendation has not been finally accepted by the highest levels of government. The NIH has suspended its support for experiments in which fetal tissue is implanted in humans. This means essentially that it has stopped the use of fetal implants in Parkinson's disease studies. But it has not stopped other laboratory research involving fetal material not transferred into humans. The Bush administration resumed the official review in 1989 but has set no deadline for reaching a decision.

NEW QUESTIONS

The furor over fetal-tissue research is a recent example of how medical technology, which is continually changing and is increasingly inventive, presents new ethical questions by pushing back the frontiers of life and death. Moral and ethical standards that served as guides for generations can be upset overnight. This happens when the answers they provide to difficult questions no longer seem relevant because of radical changes in medical technology. Consider some other historical cases:

Blood Transfusions Since the earliest times, people have regarded blood with a special reverence. It was unthinkable until very recently that one person could take and use the blood of another without grave consequences. Some religious groups, such as Jehovah's Witnesses, find using another person's blood morally repugnant and therefore forbid it.

Indeed, when doctors first began to test their ideas in this arena 300 years ago, sharing blood was a dangerous practice, and many patients who received transfusions (especially in early attempts that used animal blood) did not survive. This was before the advent of modern hygienic and sterilization practices and before

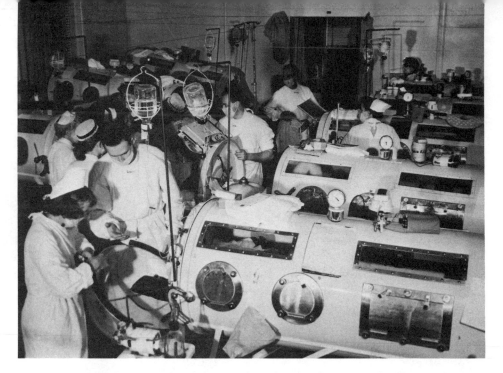

An iron lung ward in 1955. Before the development of polio vaccines in the 1950s, some victims of the disease, often children, needed an iron lung to help them breathe.

the discovery, in the early 1900s, of *blood types*. (Each person's blood carries a series of genetically determined factors—such as those of the ABO system or the Rh factor.) England, France, and Italy all outlawed transfusions for a time. But the technology has been refined, and in the United States alone 3 million people receive transfusions each year. Most of these transfusions are accomplished safely and there are few complications. Doctors not only type and match people's blood carefully but also test the blood for transmittable illnesses such as AIDS.

Ethical questions today center on who should be included in the enormous transfusion "marketplace" and on how to regulate it. Should blood banks that pay people to donate blood be allowed to operate? Is it ethical to sell blood? What are the most effective means for ensuring that the blood that people receive is as safe as possible yet ensuring the privacy of donors?

Iron Lungs and Respirators Before the 1950s, when the first effective vaccines against polio, developed by Jonas Salk and Albert Sabin, were distributed in the United States, medicine provided only half measures of help. Physicians could arrest and treat the symptoms, but a populationwide method of prevention remained out of reach. This led to the terrible spectacle of children being confined in *iron lungs*, huge cabinets that mechanically compressed the chest, making it possible for those with paralyzed lungs to breathe. This solution was so uncomfortable that some asked whether it was really preferable to death.

But the Salk and Sabin vaccines have virtually eradicated polio from the United States, and cumbersome iron lungs have been replaced by better and more flexible types of breathing apparatuses. Although science has ended the problem concerning the treatment of polio victims, there are still thousands of children who depend on respirators or other immobilizing mechanical devices for survival. In 1986, the Office of Technology Assessment, which prepares technical studies for the U.S. Congress, estimated that there were 17,000 children dependent on respirators or intravenous feeding.

One who became famous in 1988 was Natasha Herndon, a five year old in St. Louis, Missouri. Born prematurely with undeveloped lungs, she was attached early in life to a respirator and will never be able to live without it. Abandoned by her parents, she was adopted by a new family, who took her home from the hospital. When she left, the bill for her treatment stood at $2 million, illustrating another kind of ethical problem created by technology: that of the expense of high-tech care.

Should this care be limited only to the most medically needy? How do we select the most needy? The same hospital that cared for Natasha now has a three year old attached to a respirator. Her health insurance has run out, and the bill is $1.3 million and climbing. What responsibilities does society have to ensure that all citizens have reasonable access to health care, and what limits, if any, should be placed on publicly supported care?

CAT Scanners In the 1970s, the federal government tried to slow the growth of health costs by controlling the sale of an expensive new device called the *computerized axial tomography machine*, or CAT scanner. It combines a rotating X-ray camera with a computer, creating a sharp image of internal organs, a bit like a three-dimensional photo. A CAT scanner costs about $1 million. The reasons for imposing government controls was to limit the use of such specialized machines and to make more funds available for low-cost, basic health care.

The effort was partly successful. But it failed to slow the sale of CAT scanners. It ran head-on into ethical questions about why any physician should be denied one of these powerful and effective diagnostic devices. It was not clear why the government had the right to tell some doctors to share a CAT scanner instead of owning one exclusively. Is it right, doctors asked, for a planner to tell a doctor what kind of technology should be available in the doctor's office or hospital? One would think that the doctor would know best what equipment was needed. Precisely because CAT scanners worked so well, the number of buyers grew rapidly in the United States. They were commonplace by the 1980s, and hardly any U.S. hospital was without one, despite the high cost— money that could have been spent in other ways.

Since the 1970s, a new generation of even more sophisticated and costly imaging machines has been introduced to the medical world, including nuclear magnetic resonance scanners and positron-emission tomography devices. One lesson to be drawn from these developments is that technology that clearly improves the quality of medical care and the quality of life for the patient— no matter how expensive—is bound to spread rapidly across the country and make its way into most hospitals.

These cases suggest some general conclusions about the way the arrival of new technology forces people to confront ethical values. The discussion falls into two broad categories: experimental medicine and common practice.

EXPERIMENTAL MEDICINE AND COMMON PRACTICE

Questions about technology (fetal-tissue brain implants, mechanical lungs, and diagnostic scanning machines) fall into the categories of either experimental medicine or common practice. The term *experimental medicine* covers those treatments and procedures whose effectiveness has not been totally proved; thus, the government has yet to approve the procedures for general use. *Common practice* covers those treatments and procedures that are approved and regularly applied. Different standards apply in each case. Doctors using experimental procedures take bigger risks. They do not have a lot of experience with the procedures they are using; they are not sure of the risks. When they test new medicines, they first give them to patients who have little hope of recovering and so are willing to take the risk. Thus, the rules of ethical conduct in such cases are more relaxed than in regular medicine.

The main requirement is that the volunteer must understand the risks of the experiment and give consent to be part of it. This means the patient must be informed—a difficult task when doctors themselves are just learning about the treatment.

Just as technology raises questions about the use of fetal material from the "not born," an unusual experiment in New York poses a similar problem dealing with the "not dead." Physicians at the Stony Brook campus of the State University of New York reported in October 1988 that they kept the heart of a 78-year-old man beating for an hour after his death in order to test a

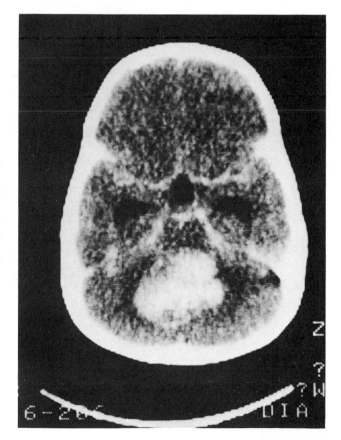

A CAT scan of a brain tumor. The CAT scanner, made widely available in the 1970s despite its $1 million cost, uses a computer and rotating X-ray camera to record an image of a specific body part.

drug. The man had been in a coma, and his relatives gave permission to use his body for research. The hospital delayed clinical death for an hour by keeping him attached to a respirator, and during this time physicians injected his body with an anticlotting drug. They wanted to observe the effects on his body before giving the drug to other patients.

In the *Annals of Internal Medicine*, they wrote that by using the dead man's body they were able to avoid exposing others to unknown dangers. They recommended this as a safe way to test drugs. But the journal's editor questioned the ethics of the experiment, saying drugs should be tested only on those who might benefit from them. This patient obviously could not. The family had given consent to use the man's body purely as an experimental tool, but the editor thought it was wrong even though the experiment was performed with the best intentions.

The big problem—as in most cases involving experimental medicine—is to get honest consent and to decide whether anyone other than the patient can give consent for such a procedure. Even though the guidelines are more relaxed in experimental cases, there are limits beyond which no ethical experiment may go. The potential for benefit must outweigh the potential for harm.

A related ethical dilemma that has stirred controversy recently is the use of animals in experiments. People have especially protested using live animals in ways that are painful or lethal to the creatures. In response, some companies that had tested products on live animals, such as some cosmetic companies, have stopped such testing. Is it ethical to raise animals strictly for experimental use? Is their use justified in some instances, such as the testing of a much-needed drug, but not in others, such as the trial of a new cosmetic? The public, along with corporations and the medical community, will have to come to a consensus on animal rights in this area.

Different problems occur in common practice. Here the whole society, not just the individual patient and doctor, has a stake in the outcome. For example, by regulating drugs the U.S. government forbids the general use of those that have not been proved safe and effective. The Food and Drug Administration (FDA) requires drug manufacturers to subject candidate medicines to trials that may take more than five years to complete. Only then, after the effects have been extensively documented, may the drugs be sold to the public, some with a doctor's prescription, others over the pharmacy counter. The FDA has set up this lengthy trial period to prevent potentially dangerous drugs from being widely distributed. A tragic example of this sort of distribution occurred in England in the 1950s: Many pregnant women were given a drug called *thalidomide* for morning sickness. The drug did help the women feel better during their pregnancies, but it caused severe deformities in their babies. Although no one would want to see an incident like the thalidomide episode occur again, there are situations involving illnesses so severe that exceptions need to be made in the drug-trial rules. The FDA did this in response to a public outcry in 1987 when it approved the anti-HIV drug *AZT* (short for azidothymidine, its original name, which has since been changed to zidovudine) after only 18 months. The first clinically useful AIDS drug, AZT was initially taken by those with full-fledged AIDS. It has been shown that people with AIDS who take it live longer than those who do not. By 1989, it was being studied to see if it would delay or prevent the onset of some of the most serious aspects of the disease if taken earlier. However, AZT has serious side effects, such as severe anemia, and about half of AIDS patients cannot tolerate it—so the search for AIDS drugs continues.

In the same way that society controls drugs, it also may wish to limit the use of certain kinds of medical equipment. It wants good evidence that a new device, such as an artificial heart, provides safe and effective therapy for the average patient before allowing its sale. It may be better to hold off on general distribution of a new technology until improvements are made. For example, it is debatable whether certain machines such as iron lungs or artificial hearts improved the quality of life for those who were attached to them. The government at present has not entirely ruled out the use of artificial hearts, but it has said that they need to be improved before being included in the general practice of medicine.

Ethical standards are stricter and more controversial when they involve the public at large than when they are in a controlled experiment. Often the key issue boils down to this: Is the tech-

A 1988 demonstration in Boston urged greater availability of the drug pentamadine, which helps prevent pneumonia in AIDS patients. In 1987, similar protests had helped convince the FDA to shorten the trial period for AZT.

nology good enough to be given to the public? Has it proved its value? To find an answer, one must weigh many kinds of evidence: information on effectiveness, on the quality of life, and on cost.

THE FUTURE

Although one cannot predict the future, it seems clear that certain ethical issues will be important later. Clinics testing AIDS drugs such as AZT have encountered problems because patients are asking the government to take a new approach. Because of the severity of the disease, they do not want to wait for the approval process to take its normal, slow course. In that time, an AIDS patient may well die. Such a delay in the drug approval process is unethical, they say. Instead, they want to cut testing short, as was done for AZT, and make every new drug that comes along available for AIDS victims.

This seems like a reasonable request, and the FDA seems to agree in part. The agency has sped up its approval process and is looking for ways to speed it up further. Still, there are some difficult technical and ethical roadblocks to such changes.

If experiments are cut short, researchers will be unable to find a definitive answer to questions about a new drug's safety or efficacy. This could result in the sale of relatively useless or dangerous but expensive medicines that raise the hopes of those with the deadly disease.

To get a valid test result, one must compare one group of patients taking the drug (the test group) with another group not taking it (the control group). This can be done in one of two ways: *blind*, which means that the subjects of the experiment are not told who is in the control group or who is in the test group; or *double-blind*, which means that neither the doctors nor the subjects know who is in which group. Both of these techniques eliminate physical effects that stem from a psychological basis— that is, a person who knows he or she is not receiving the drug may become depressed, and this depression may cause the person to lose hope, allowing the physical condition to worsen. *Placebos*, or inert substances in the form of medication, may be given in either case to make it impossible to tell which group is receiving the drug.

Some AIDS victims may not want to join a drug experiment for fear that they will be part of the control rather than the test group. But if no one will join an experiment with a control group, there can be no comparison, and it may take longer to decide which drugs work. Some researchers are concerned that the drive to speed up the approval of AIDS drugs will affect other drug tests, resulting in a general decline in drug safety. Should any patient have to join a control group if he or she does not want to? Is it more important to respond to the AIDS emergency by releasing drugs quickly, or is it necessary to maintain the highest standards of drug testing, even if it means that some patients in control groups will risk not getting a valuable medicine? These points are now being debated.

Another problem concerning medications has to do with vaccines. Wealthy industrial countries can afford to offer vaccines to protect children against lethal diseases. Smallpox, yellow fever, and typhoid have all but vanished in these areas. But children of poorer nations, especially in the tropics, are not so fortunate. Likewise, there are many diseases that cannot be vaccinated against but which are easily treatable with antibiotics. According to the U.S. Institute of Medicine, diarrhea caused by the *Shigella* bacterium may sicken as many as 250 million children a year and kill 654,000. Streptococcal pneumonia may afflict 100 million and kill 10 million annually.

Whereas in some cases a country may lack the money to provide an already developed vaccine or antibiotic, in other cases a new vaccine needs to be created. In a November 1988 article in *Scientific American*, "Obstacles to Developing Vaccines for the Third World," medical experts Anthony Robbins and Phyllis Freeman write that it is not a lack of knowledge that makes it difficult to create vaccines against these diseases so much as it is a lack of money. Drug manufacturers have little incentive to invest in such work because the profits to be made are small. The poorer nations simply cannot afford to pay the high initial price that is charged for new vaccines. And so vaccines are not developed. To break the logjam, governments of developing countries could invest directly in new vaccine research. But the countries that most need the vaccines often do not have any sophisticated pharmaceutical makers within their borders.

Should the developing nations pay profit-making companies in Europe or the United States to develop the needed vaccines? But these Third World governments ask themselves, why not try to find an agency that will develop the vaccines cheaply, without asking for a profit? If the research effort is successful, should drug companies be allowed to keep control of the technology? Should profits be shared between the company and the country that funded it? These are just a few of the vexing questions that will confront international medical agencies as they try to remedy the lack of investment in vaccines for poor nations.

The World Health Organization has suggested in "TDR and the Dry Industries" in the magazine of the WHO, that a special institute could be set up for vaccine development. It could be funded from a combination of public and private sources. This is one possible solution to the problems of poor countries needing medical developments for which they are unable to pay, but it is not yet a reality.

One of the most exciting and controversial new areas of biology concerns human genetics. Each human being's cells contain a set of 46 *chromosomes*, 23 from the person's mother and 23 from the person's father. These chromosomes contain *genes* for all inherited traits, such as gender, eye color, and hair color. These genes are composed of *DNA*, or deoxyribonucleic acid, a complex

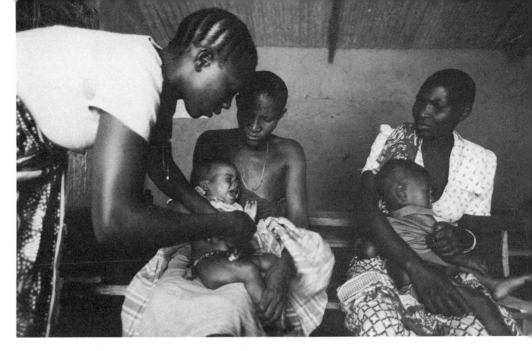

A health-care worker vaccinates a child in Tanzania. Lack of available vaccines in Third World countries causes a serious problem: Millions die every year from diseases that rarely affect people in developed countries.

molecule whose structure was not even identified until 1953. By the late 1980s, researchers were well on their way to unraveling the entire *genetic code*, the set of operating instructions for the human body. It is estimated that every human carries a set of 100,000 genes; researchers have thus far identified 1,500 of them.

Genes determine the development of individual features, as well as the lungs, brain, bones, tissue, and other organs. When defective, however, they also cause illness or birth defects. There are thought to be hundreds of genetic disorders. Some are relatively common, such as *sickle-cell anemia*, a blood disorder that affects some people of African heritage, or *Tay-Sachs disease*, which is found among Jewish families. Researchers have been able to connect a specific gene with a specific disease in only a few of these cases. And even when the identity of the gene is known, its location on a chromosome is not. Thus, although scientists are rapidly assembling the puzzle of gene-based diseases, many pieces are missing.

Even at this early stage of research, however, ethical issues have appeared. One question that hangs over the field is whether it is right for humans to change their own genetic code. Is it right to tinker with the fundamental elements of life, perhaps to change the very shape of the human form? At this time, the question is an abstract one, because the scientific community's skills in genetic engineering are not good enough to redesign the genetic code. Nonetheless, some experiments are edging toward this possibility.

At NIH, the question arose in 1988 as to whether it would be permissible to inject some genes from a bacterium into a human blood cell and then inject the blood cells into cancer patients. The research team, lead by Steven A. Rosenberg and R. Michael Blaese of the National Cancer Institute and W. French Anderson of the National Heart, Lung, and Blood Institute, wanted to use the bacterial gene as a marker, an identifiable element that could be used to track a cell. It would be attached to a type of blood cell that researchers hoped would seek out and attack tumors. By following the marked cells as they went through the body, researchers would be able to discover whether the blood cells were doing their job properly. Although this did not involve changing human genes at all, researchers at NIH hesitated and studied the question for months before going forward with the experiment in 1989.

The momentous step will come when some researcher attempts to perform gene therapy. This will involve replacing a defective gene with a healthy one. There are, of course, technical risks in doing this: If the genetic implant itself proves defective, the patient may suffer permanent injury or death.

Quite apart from the technical risk, however, is the problem of distinguishing what is ethically acceptable from what is not. Today, most people seem to agree that it would be wrong to tinker with human genes; for example, to make an ordinary person stronger or smarter. At the same time, many feel that it would be proper to change a person's genes to halt the effects of a disease such as sickle-cell anemia. Somewhere in between creating supermen and eradicating disease, society will draw a line delineating what doctors may and may not do. The task of defining the line will occupy ethicists for years to come.

•   •   •   •

CHAPTER 3

HIGH-TECH SEXUAL REPRODUCTION

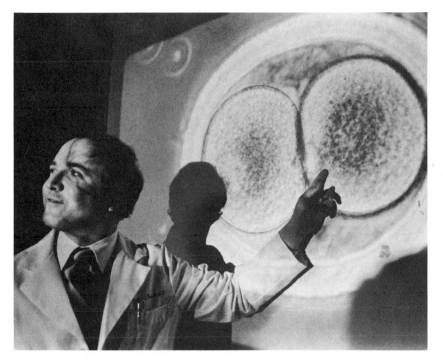

Zygote created through in vitro fertilization

Like all other areas of medicine, reproductive science has seen drastic changes and advances since the start of the 20th century. These changes have redefined some very basic concepts: what it means to be a mother or a father, the point at which life begins. In the field of genetics, the advances have been great but are surely only the beginning. The future holds possibilities ranging from the exciting prospect of curing genetic diseases and birth defects to the frightening possibility of parents voluntarily designing the genes of their offspring or, even worse, having someone else design them. The following case histories illustrate two of the new technologies and some of the problems that can stem from their use.

CASE ONE: THE RIOS FAMILY

Mario and Elsa Rios, a wealthy couple living in Los Angeles, wanted to have a child but were unable to do so because Mario, then 50 years old, was not fertile. In 1981, they went to Melbourne, Australia, seeking help from the world-renowned fertility clinic of the Victoria Medical Center. It performs in vitro fertilization, a procedure in which sperm taken from a man and eggs from a woman are put in a laboratory dish. They join to make fertilized eggs that develop into *pre-embryos*, one of which is selected and placed back in the woman's uterus, in the hope that it will grow into a normal child. The others are frozen for later use or disposed of. In the Rios case, the sperm came from an anonymous Australian and the eggs from Elsa Rios, then age 37.

The operation succeeded, but Elsa miscarried and lost the child. She decided not to try again right away. Then tragedy struck. Elsa and Mario died in a plane crash in Chile in 1983.

Soon, the Melbourne clinic declared that it wanted to implant the remaining Rios pre-embryos in another woman. But a question arose because Mario and Elsa Rios had died without a will: Who would inherit their wealth? Would it go to the child born from their frozen pre-embryos? In the end, a California court ruled that it would not; as far as the court was concerned the pre-embryos were not living people. In any case, the pre-embryos, which were frozen in 1981 when procedures were less sophisticated, would probably not survive being thawed so it is unlikely that they will be implanted in another woman.

CASE TWO: BABY M

William and Elizabeth Stern, a professional couple in New Jersey, wanted a family, but Elizabeth was unable to bear children. They went to the Infertility Center of New York, which recruited a *surrogate mother* to help them—a woman named Mary Beth

Whitehead. She agreed to be artificially inseminated with sperm from William Stern (*artificial insemination* is the implantation of sperm into a woman's cervix without sexual intercourse), and the Sterns agreed to pay her $10,000 to deliver a baby for them.

The procedure worked well, and a healthy girl (named Melissa by the Sterns, Sara by Mary Beth Whitehead, and called Baby M in court papers) was born in 1986. Whitehead asked to keep Baby M for a few days. Suddenly, she ran away to Florida, refusing to give the child to the Sterns.

William Stern, who had already paid the $10,000, obtained a court order granting him custody of Baby M, based on the surrogate motherhood contract. The court agreed. It ordered Whitehead to turn the baby over to Stern in 1987 and denied her the right to visit the child. Elizabeth Stern became the legal mother by adoption.

A year later, the New Jersey Supreme Court overturned part of this decision. According to the court, the contract was invalid because it violated a state law against baby selling. Mary Beth Whitehead-Gould (she had divorced and remarried by this time) was the true mother, the court said, and like any other, she should be allowed to visit her daughter. But it did not overrule the earlier decision that gave custody of the child to the Sterns. The court felt that it would be harmful to the child to uproot her after living with the Sterns for a year and a half. Mary Beth Whitehead-Gould was granted "unsupervised, uninterrupted, liberal visitation" rights.

THE SEXUAL REVOLUTION CONTINUES

These cases are but two of the controversies that have come about as a result of what has been a revolution concerning human conception and childbirth in this century. The revolution began with the birth control pill, which freed women from the biological imperative of childbirth. It became possible to avoid having children, if desired, by simply taking a pill every day. *Amniocentesis*, a method of testing for genetic defects before birth, is one of many new procedures that give parents more information about the embryo at an early stage. This knowledge, combined with sophisticated medical procedures and—at least between the 1973

55

decision in *Roe v. Wade* and the 1989 reconsideration of this decision in several cases, including *Webster v. Reproductive Health Services*—the legality of abortion, enable parents to make an informed decision to terminate a pregnancy before term when a child is unwanted or is believed to have a genetic defect.

New technology also makes it possible for many couples who thought they would never have children to do so, and this has multiplied the choices and questions—medical, legal, and ethical—surrounding reproduction. As new situations come to light, society tries to develop new standards to deal with them. But the changes are occurring so quickly that society is hard-pressed to keep ethical standards as sophisticated as the medical choices people confront.

The main force creating new reproductive technology today is the desire to help couples have children. The Office of Technology Assessment reported in 1988 that there were 2 to 3 million American couples who wanted to have a baby but could not do so without medical help. Americans spend about $1 billion a year seeking such help. Because the demand is so strong, physicians

Liquid nitrogen is used to freeze sperm stored in sperm banks such as this one in California, which is a repository for the sperm of Nobel laureates. Sperm banks for the purpose of artificial insemination have been in existence since the 1950s; more recently, donated sperm has also been used for in vitro fertilization.

Amniocentesis and Gender in India

Maharashtra, a state in western India, decided in 1988 to make it illegal for parents to use amniocentesis to find out the sex of a child. Amniocentesis has become a common prenatal test, used in the United States primarily by women over age 35, who run a higher risk of conceiving a child with genetic defects. The test involves removing fluid from the amniotic sac with a needle and then analyzing chromosomes from the baby's cells found in the fluid for signs of genetic problems. Its main purpose is to detect Down's syndrome—a type of retardation caused by the presence of an extra chromosome. As it happens, the test also reveals the baby's sex. If the fetus is found to have Down's syndrome, parents often seek an abortion. In India, parents also frequently ask for an abortion if they learn the fetus is female. To stop this practice, the state outlawed the use of such testing to determine gender—although it could continue to be used to check for Down's syndrome.

One reason for India's bias against girls is that they are expensive. By tradition, the parents must provide a generous dowry to the husband at marriage, often $10,000—which is frequently the equivalent of a year's salary.

One doctor who performed such abortions, Sharad Gogate, spoke to the *New York Times*. He described a woman who had four daughters and then learned from amniocentesis that she was about to have a fifth. Gogate said, "This woman cried and cried because her husband was going to throw her out of the house if she failed to produce a son." At her request, Gogate performed an abortion. In 1986, Gogate helped 25 to 30 women each week to have such abortions. He was ordered to stop but said other physicians would continue. The *Times* reported that tens of thousands of abortions like this have occurred in recent years. Now, following Maharashtra's example, India is considering a national ban on the use of amniocentesis to determine sex.

have been encouraged to experiment with the basic elements of life to create new methods of reproduction.

It has been possible for many years to transfer sperm artificially from a man to a woman. Sperm can also be stored for later use by freezing it in superchilled gas—a process called *cryopreservation*. In this way, clinics can maintain *sperm banks* containing sperm cells from a great number of potential fathers. It is also possible to take an egg from a woman's body and fertilize it with sperm from the bank, and then freeze the partially developed pre-embryo, to be placed later in a woman's uterus. (Unfertilized eggs are more fragile and more difficult to preserve.) Louise Brown, the first test-tube baby (a baby conceived through in vitro fertilization and then implanted in a woman's uterus), was born in England in 1978. Since then, an estimated 4,000 to 5,000 children worldwide have been conceived this way.

It may not be long before clinics store frozen sperm, eggs, and pre-embryos. It is no fantasy to imagine a world in which clients shop at a clinic, looking not just for a baby but, say, a girl with dark hair, green eyes, and Mediterranean heritage.

THE RIGHT TO CONCEIVE— OR NOT TO CONCEIVE

Medically aided reproduction is inevitably accompanied by ethical issues. What claims do donors of sperm and eggs have on the pre-embryos made from them? What are the limits on biological parenthood? What about embryos? At what point are they to be treated as people, possessed of legal rights even though they are unborn?

The due process clause of the Fifth Amendment to the U.S. Constitution has been extended to protect a married couple's right to use contraceptives (*Griswold v. Connecticut*, 1965); this same amendment may be taken to protect a couple's right to procreate, regardless of the means by which the child is conceived. However, state and federal governments may control business transactions, and it is permissible under the Constitution to outlaw the sale of reproductive services. This has not happened on a national scale as yet, although some states are moving in this direction. For example, New Jersey prohibited paid surrogacy after the Baby M case.

At present, there are few controls on the fertility industry, although, as shown in the Baby M case, there are laws against baby selling. It is possible that such controls may be extended to certain practices now on the fringe of legality, such as surrogacy and *embryo transfer* (the sperm of a man is used to fertilize an egg in a woman's reproductive system, after which the fertilized egg is removed and implanted in the man's partner). Human sperm has been available since 1950 from sperm banks; after some initial controversy the use of sperm banks has become common practice, and no move has been made to end such sales. It seems well established. But questions seem to arise when a child or an embryo is separated from its biological mother. At least two states (Florida and Louisiana) already have specifically outlawed the sale of pre-embryos, and many are considering a ban on payment for surrogate motherhood. Forbidding the sale of pre-embryos or surrogate motherhood services would not make it illegal to have children by these means. But it would limit such practices because few people, donors or surrogates, would be willing to make the emotional investment in a fertility program if there were no reward for themselves. Out of sympathy for relatives or friends, people no doubt would continue to donate reproductive material, just as they donate blood or kidneys. But with the lure of money removed, such donations would be exceptional. Many ethicists believe this might be a good result.

Carole Jalbert (right) holds the baby her sister, Sherry King (left), bore for her. If paid surrogacy agreements are made illegal, family arrangements such as this might be one of the only types to continue.

Clinics that perform in vitro fertilization are regarded as being engaged in experimental medicine for an initial period after they set up operations. Those that have a record of success are seen as doing standard medicine by the government regulators. In 1988, there were fewer than 200 IVF clinics in the United States. They are governed by the same ethical rules that apply to other types of specialized medicine. Two major concerns are the possibilities for quackery, or use of "medical" practices that are of no benefit, and the unscrupulous use of patients. Infertile couples, in their desperate search for help, may become the victims of "experts" making promises they cannot keep while charging thousands of dollars in consulting fees, or they may be pressured into giving up rights to reproductive materials on which the clinic can make a profit.

The rate of success in fertility therapy is quite low. The best IVF clinics report that only 10% of patients conceive a child as a result of therapy. Some figures indicate the national success rate is far lower. Because failure is so common, incompetence and fraud are easy to conceal; only the most knowledgeable clients could tell the difference between a good attempt that failed and a bad attempt that never had a chance of succeeding.

There is a lot of interest among medical researchers in experimenting with embryonic material, especially to improve methods of IVF. Parents may come under subtle pressure from the clinic to agree to donate their unused pre-embryos to the clinic for its own use. It is important for patients to know that not all clinics make this request. As in other fields of experimental medicine, patients should be fully informed of the chances of failure (90% in the case of IVF) and the risks of complications.

Patients who do not use their own eggs or their own sperm should also know something about the donors of sperm or eggs they receive. It is vitally important, for example, to know whether the donor was a victim of AIDS, for this fatal disease can be passed on to offspring and to the mother at the time of insemination. In October 1989, New York State became the first state to pass a law that determined a sperm donor's eligibility. To help guard against AIDS transmission through anonymously donated sperm, the New York State Health Department now requires the donor to undergo two AIDS tests six months apart and asks that any man who has had homosexual sex since 1977 not donate. In

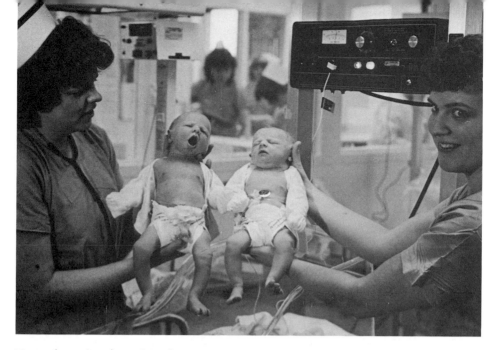

Test-tube twins, born in February 1984. An increasing number of couples with fertility problems are conceiving by artificial means.

addition to information about AIDS, parents may also want general information such as the racial identity or other characteristics of the donor.

But the fertility clinic is also bound to protect the confidentiality of donors. Therefore it must walk a narrow line between openness and privacy. Although some adopted children have argued that they have a right to know the names of their biological parents, state courts generally have not agreed. At present, it seems unlikely that fertility clinic patients will be entitled to obtain much more than general information about the source of donated sperm and eggs. It also seems unlikely that children born by IVF at present have any claim to know who donated the sperm or eggs from which they were born—unless, of course, the donors were their own parents.

Do sperm and egg donors have any lasting ownership of the material they have given? Can they claim any right to custody of the children? In general, the answer is no. Donors surrender their parental role at the time they give the material to the fertility clinic. Laws in 30 states dealing with sperm banks make this rule clear: Donors have no right to custody or to visit any children born of their sperm. They also have no obligation to provide child support. The same principle will probably be applied to eggs and pre-embryos, although it is impossible to predict how the courts will regard them. Society treats the mother-child bond as sacred, and it may honor biological claims to fertilized eggs more than it has honored the claims of sperm donors.

Some new rulings on other medical cases, however, may affect standards in reproductive medicine. John Moore, a leukemia patient in California, successfully sued his physicians over the use of tissue they removed from his spleen during an operation in 1976. Even though he agreed to donate the tissue to research at the time of his therapy, he did not realize it would be used to create a profitable medicine. After learning many years later that a patented drug had been made from cells taken from his body, he demanded a share of the profits.

Eventually, Moore won a hearing in the California Court of Appeals. But before the case went to trial, the physicians agreed to share the income with him. Some think the precedent set by this case could expand the "property" rights of sperm, egg, and embryo donors.

Hardly any subject in medicine has received more attention or provoked more controversy in the last 30 years than the legal status of the "unborn." The debate has to do with when an embryo becomes entitled to legal rights and when a woman may ask a physician to abort a developing embryo. In 1973, the debate intensified when the U.S. Supreme Court decided in *Roe v. Wade* that abortion may not be outlawed during the first three months, or first trimester, of pregnancy. (Individual states had the right to outlaw abortion before this ruling.) The Court said a woman's right to privacy includes the right to control her own body during these early weeks of pregnancy.

However, the Court added that as the embryo grows, it begins to develop a life of its own and rights of its own. At the age of 24 to 28 weeks, the fetus is "viable" outside the mother and so deserves protection. To protect the fetus, the Court ruled, states may outlaw abortion in the last trimester of pregnancy, after the 24th week. In the second trimester (12th to 24th week), the Court said, states may regulate abortion only to protect the mother's health, not the fetus's. The effect of the decision was to make abortions legal for those who could afford them.

The aim was to give a woman the right to make decisions

regarding her own body and also to protect new human beings, but this is a complex issue because there are no exact scientific lines that mark the moment when sperm and egg become human. The matter is highly debatable. Although many felt the *Roe* decision had settled the issue, this was not so. Throughout the 1970s and 1980s, many other abortion issues were brought before the courts: whether a minor needed the permission of one or both of her parents before she could have an abortion, whether Medicaid would pay for poor women's abortions, and whether a man whose partner was seeking an abortion had any say in the matter. The social climate in the United States and the makeup of the Supreme Court changed during the years of Ronald Reagan's presidency (1981–89), and a highly organized and vocal anti-abortion movement gained power. In 1989, the Supreme Court elected to hear a case, *Webster v. Reproductive Health Services*, that threatened to overturn *Roe v. Wade*.

The *Webster* case mobilized forces on both sides of the issue. On April 9, more than 300,000 people turned out to participate in a prochoice march in Washington, D.C. In response, anti-abortion groups filled an area near the Capitol with white crosses, each representing a baby that was aborted. On July 3, 1989, by a 5–4 vote, the Supreme Court upheld the Missouri court's decision to allow that state to restrict abortion. The Missouri law forbids abortion at publicly financed medical units, bars federal employees from participating in abortions not necessary to save the life of the mother, and bars use of any federal buildings for that purpose. Although the *Webster* decision did not completely overturn *Roe v. Wade*, it considerably weakened it.

The Supreme Court has agreed to hear three other abortion cases during the 1989–90 session: *Ohio v. Akron Center for Reproductive Health*, *Hodgson v. Minnesota*, and *Turnock v. Ragsdale*. The first two cases concern requiring minors seeking abortions to notify their parents—*Ohio* would call for notification of one parent, *Hodgson* would require that of both parents (even if the parents were never married, are divorced, or if the father is also the incestuous father of the fetus). *Turnock* involves an Illinois law requiring private abortion clinics (which, as of 1985, performed 60% of U.S. abortions) to meet standards imposed on full-care hospital operating rooms. If the Court rules in favor of Illinois in this case, those abortion clinics that are not

The controversy over abortion has sparked intense emotions on both sides of the issue, as this photo of a 1984 confrontation in Boston, Massachusetts, demonstrates.

forced out of business would be forced to raise their prices significantly to provide for the new facilities. Although decisions further restricting abortion rights in these cases might leave abortion technically legal, the reality would be a two-tiered system in which the rich might have the right to choose but the poor would be left with few options. In upcoming years, people will have to decide if this is fair. No doubt, there will be more challenges to what is left of the *Roe* decision. The decisions of the Supreme Court will be pivotal, but no more so than what happens state by state in the legislatures. The citizens of the United States will help decide this issue through local elections and grass-roots organizations.

The debate is far from over, and it has implications for other areas in medicine, such as IVF therapy. Some of the same questions come up because in IVF more pre-embryos are created than are used. Should the "spares" that are not used be kept in the lab for later use? Should they be regarded as people, entitled to the protection of the Constitution? Should they be treated in a manner similar to sperm? Is it ethically acceptable to give them to other, unrelated "parents"? Is it all right to discard them?

There is no clear consensus among ethicists or legal experts as to how to treat pre-embryos. But there seems to be an inclination to treat them as "more human" than sperm or unfertilized eggs because they are potentially complete human beings. Pre-embryos are thus more than a standard medical commodity. Yet, as the Rios case shows, they are not seen as having the full legal rights of humans.

Although there may be no agreement, it is possible to suggest some basic standards for dealing with pre-embryos. The Office of Technology Assessment describes a few ethical rules adopted in 1986 by the American Fertility Society (AFS), an organization that serves as a professional forum for people interested in the problems of infertility and methods of alleviating them. The AFS recommended that

- Pre-embryos should not be preserved in the lab after the death of the woman who donated the eggs.
- Pre-embryos should not be kept for any purpose other than the one for which they were originally donated.
- Pre-embryos should not be transferred from one generation to another, that is, from mother to daughter.
- Parents should be consulted before they donate sperm or eggs and should approve the final disposition of pre-embryos (that is, the donor should give informed permission for the use of his or her reproductive materials).

BRAVE NEW WORLD

One question that may sound simple but is very hard to answer concerns a child's right to have a so-called normal childhood. Women may choose to bear children without ever marrying, or, for that matter, without sexual contact with a man. These women can have children through such clinical procedures as artificial insemination or IVF. Does society have any responsibility to the offspring of this new technology? Should families seeking embryonic material have to meet a test of eligibility? Is there any ethical basis for denying single women, or gay couples, the privilege of using IVF? Is it fair to permit the wealthy to use artificial insemination but to deny access to the poor? There are no easy answers.

The questions raised by IVF and other new technologies, strange as they may seem, are the beginning of a new age in human reproduction. If the dreams of bioengineers come true, science will soon uncover the finest details in the structure of human life. The government is already making a large investment in "mapping" the entire human genetic code. The expectation is that by the beginning of the 21st century, every gene in the huge complex that defines the human being will have been discovered and recorded in computer files. Scientists may be able to say exactly which pieces of the genetic code make blue or brown eyes or turn hair curly or straight. The possibilities are enormous, leading perhaps to a world in which children will be "designed" as well as conceived by their parents. This potential seems morally repugnant to many, especially when viewed against the backdrop of Nazi Germany's eugenics experiments or of some ancient civilizations' use of infanticide as a means of eugenics.

Some ethicists fear society is moving rapidly down a path that will degrade respect for human life. If qualities in a child can be defined chemically, selected by computer, and bought for a fee, how will that affect people's feelings for their fellow humans? Will life lose some of its integrity? Or will the power to control inherited qualities, including disease, enable people to define humanity even better? Will it perhaps make them even "more human"?

At times, questions like these sound abstract. But, as a careful reading of almost any week's newspapers reveals, they are not so far removed from what is happening in the laboratory. The answers found for today's hypothetical questions will become tomorrow's public policy.

•   •   •   •

CHAPTER 4

THE ETHICS OF
ORGAN
TRANSPLANTATION

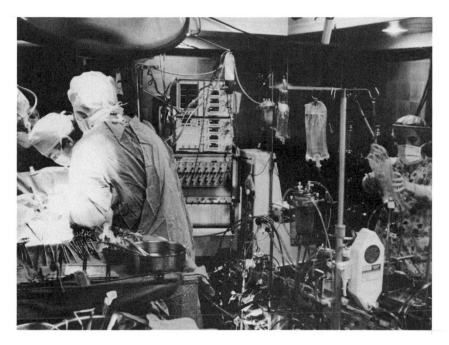

Heart transplant surgery

Doctors performed the first kidney transplant in 1954, the first heart transplant and the first lung transplant in 1967, and the first heart-and-lung transplant in 1981. These achievements have brought with them a whole series of ethical questions. On what basis, for example, should those waiting for organs be wait listed? What restrictions should be placed on the solicitation of organ donations from family members of a recently deceased prospective donor? Although this new technology may save many lives, there is—as in the case of many medical advances—a potential for abuse.

DEATH ON THE SIDEWALK

In April 1988, police officers in Costa Mesa, California, found an unconscious young man on the sidewalk in front of a convenience store. They could not revive him, so they took him to a nearby hospital—the Hoag Medical Center. That Tuesday morning when they dropped him off, they had no idea who he was. They tried to locate his family, but he was unconscious and had no identification. The police did not know where to turn.

The next day, the hospital found that the young man's brain showed no signs of electrical activity; it was therefore dead. That afternoon, doctors removed his heart for transplantation. In a short time, his healthy heart was implanted in the chest of Dr. Norton Humphreys, a 58-year-old physician, formerly of the Hoag Center staff, whose own heart was diseased and failing.

The day after the operation, a family called the police to report that their 19-year-old boy was missing. His name was Eleno Ulloa Ramirez, they said, and they gave police a photo and an ID card that allowed him to work in the United States. When the police saw the photo, they recognized him as the same young man they had picked up on the sidewalk two days earlier. The Ramirez case sent a shock through the medical community because it vividly displayed some of the problems in organ transplantation. Doctors almost never use the body of an unidentified person as an organ donor, and several experts in medical ethics said they thought the hospital acted too hastily.

On the other hand, as the hospital staff said, Ramirez was legally dead when the operation was performed. He may have died of a drug overdose, for there were traces of cocaine and alcohol in his urine. An effort was made to find relatives or friends, as the state's Uniform Anatomical Gift Act requires, but none were found. According to law, if the police try to identify a body of a dead person and fail, after 24 hours the organs may be removed for transplant. Thus, the hospital staff felt it had not only followed the rules but had done something good by using Ramirez's heart to save a life.

The Ramirez case highlighted the intense demand for healthy organs. It pointed out the tendency of well-to-do patients to benefit from transplants more often than the poor did. And it hinted at a nightmare of possibilities that could occur if there were no ethical guidelines on how to proceed.

THE GROWING DEMAND FOR "USED" ORGANS

The number of doctors who can perform transplants and the variety of organs that can be transplanted have both expanded tremendously since the first kidney transplant was done in 1954. This growth in expertise has led to increasing competition for "spare" human parts. The Ramirez case is an unusual example of what can happen as a result of this increased demand.

More often, doctors are reluctant to remove organs; frequently, out of concern for the grieving family's feelings, they do not even ask for permission to do so. This creates an unfortunate situation. Even though deaths that leave usable organs are common, more people need transplants than there are available organs. According to the American Council on Transplantation, there are an estimated 20,000 to 25,000 *brain deaths* (deaths from damage to the brain leaving organs intact and usable) each year in the United States, but only 20% are organ donors. The supply could be adequate if more individuals would carry donor cards or if more families would donate organs of relatives at death. According to the American Society of Transplant Surgeons, only 10% of the organs that could be used for transplantation are made available.

A survey reported in a June 1985 *Journal of the American Medical Association* article, "Public Attitudes and Behavior Regarding Organ Donation," revealed that people seem to be divided in their thinking about organ transplants. Although the overwhelming majority of those polled (94%) had heard about the need for organ donations, and half (50%) said they were willing to donate their organs at death, relatively few (28%) said they would carry a card identifying themselves as willing to donate. Even fewer (19%) said they actually carried such a card.

But although donors are hard to find, medical advances have made the actual transplantation of organs a more common operation. One reason is a new drug called *cyclosporine*, a chemical that controls some aspects of the immune system. Just as the factors in blood make it impossible to give a person a transfusion of blood with a different set of factors, tissue and organs need to be matched, or typed. Factors in the blood and components of organs or tissues act as *antigens*, triggering production of *antibodies*, molecules that combat foreign, usually harmful cells or other material. Cyclosporine works by inhibiting the function of one type of immune system cell, *T cells*, which regulate antibody production. This makes it much less likely that a person's body will reject a transplanted organ as foreign, thus making it easier to match available organs with needy patients. After the FDA approved cyclosporine in November 1983, it became widely available. New drugs and organ-preservation techniques are now becoming available, and this will make it even easier in the 1990s to transplant organs from one body to another.

A London surgeon talks to his patient four days after kidney transplant surgery. First performed in 1954, kidney transplants have helped many people resume a normal life.

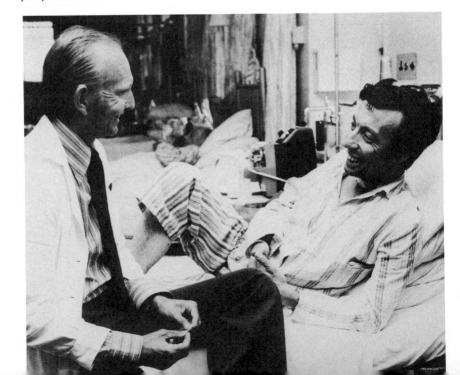

In the 1980s, the number of transplants performed in the United States rose by nearly 100%—from fewer than 5,000 in 1981 to more than 9,000 in 1987. The number of heart transplants in this period grew 20 times and liver transplants, 30 times. This was possible because of cyclosporine and other medical developments, such as improvement in surgical procedures and better methods of tissue typing. Medical procedures of this kind are rapidly moving out of the experimental category and into the class of routine practice. (Insurers, however, still seek to limit the growth of the practice by labeling such cases "experimental.")

But advances aside, the fact remains that there are many fewer available organs than patients who need them. In recent years the supply of available organs has fallen so far behind demand that up to 12,000 people in the United States are waiting for a transplant, according to current estimates. The shortfall sometimes drives aggressive physicians and patients searching for organs to take questionable steps.

Buying and Selling Organs

In procuring organs, U.S. physicians have followed the rule that it is best to get organs from "cadaveric" sources, or dead bodies. This approach helps reduce the number of cases in which a person might come under strong pressure to donate a kidney to a friend or relative. (A person can live and function with only one kidney, so it is possible for a living person to be a kidney donor.) And it reduces the likelihood that anyone could find a secret black market where it would be possible to buy human kidneys, for example, from live people who need the money.

It is interesting to see how different cultures live by different ethical standards, in medicine as in many other aspects of life. The policy on transplantation in India, for example, is the complete opposite of that in the United States. In India it is illegal to take organs from the dead. This means that not only are friends and relatives called on to make sacrifices but so are complete strangers.

According to *Nature* magazine (1987), "trading in live human kidneys has become big business in Bombay. Entrepreneurs will offer a package deal on transplant services—a kidney and the necessary surgery—for prices ranging between £4,800 and

£72,000. . . . Typically agents hunt for poor migrant laborers willing to give up a kidney" for a small fee. To control the practice, *Nature* reports, the local state council decided to impose a new law that requires all donors and recipients to be interviewed by a panel of experts before the operation is approved.

Shortages and problems in organ procurement—though none quite as dramatic as in the case of Bombay—began to surface in the United States in the 1980s. To bring the situation under control, Congress enacted the National Organ Transplant Act of 1984. This law prohibits the sale of any human organs for profit and establishes a network of government-supported organ procurement centers around the nation. Its goal is to educate the public about the need for organ donations and speed up the tissue-matching procedure. It is also aimed at preventing the creation of a commodities market for human organs.

A Controversial Experiment

One attempt to find a new source of organs in 1987 at the Loma Linda Medical Center near Los Angeles provoked a national controversy. This had to do with sustaining the lives of anencephalic newborns, infants who fail to develop a higher (fully developed) brain in the womb. About 3,000 such children are born each year in the United States, and they usually die shortly after birth.

Rather than let them die immediately, however, Loma Linda began to keep them alive long enough to find another child who needed a transplant. (The anencephalic infants had to be kept alive until the last possible moment because their organs quickly deteriorate after they die.) As soon as a candidate recipient could be found, Loma Linda's staff removed the anencephalic child from the life support system and let death take its course. The organs were then transplanted.

Although the procedure may have saved the life of at least one child (a Canadian named Paul Holc), it raised so many ethical questions that the hospital suspended the practice after less than one year. Loma Linda also backed off because it proved technically difficult to keep anencephalic children hovering between life and death, and sometimes—after being kept alive on the

A couple holds a photo-graph of their eight-week-old daughter, who needs a liver transplant. Anencephalic babies kept alive at Los Ange-les's Loma Linda Medical Center provided organ donations for some such infants.

respirator—they seemed to live longer than those who were not kept alive artificially.

Critics felt that keeping anencephalic babies alive just for the purpose of taking their organs demeaned the dignity of life. One article blasted the practice as "out-Heroding Herod"—a reference to the biblical story of the Roman ruler who ordered all male infants of a certain age killed.

Some objected on a less emotional basis to Loma Linda's ex-periment, saying the procedure caused these children to live longer and thus prolonged their suffering. Others saw it as a dangerous first step toward a system that would use comatose patients, deeply retarded children, and even the incurably insane as disposable medical property.

Because of these problems, the hospital decided to give up on organ procurement from anencephalic babies, even though it also meant giving up on saving the lives of some desperately needy children. They felt it was more important to maintain an ethical standard in this case than to take the extreme measures that were necessary to save lives.

WHO SHOULD RECEIVE ORGANS?

Equally difficult problems come up at the receiving end of the system, for doctors must decide who among a large number of waiting patients will be first to get a new organ when it becomes available. With 12,000 people now in line, it is inevitable that some decisions will seem unfair, no matter how carefully they are made.

Under the National Organ Transplant Act, the single standard for allocating organs in the United States is medical need. In some countries, including Britain, transplants are not performed on the older patients, on the grounds that the precious gift of life should be given first to those who can make the most use of it—the young and otherwise strong. But in the United States, the medically neediest patient has the highest claim, regardless of when he or she first got in line and regardless of age.

A *New York Times* reporter on a visit to the heart transplant center at Columbia-Presbyterian Hospital in New York City noted that the two newest additions to the waiting line were middle-aged men. They were both former heavy (three-packs-a-day) smokers who had damaged their heart with nicotine use and excessive carbon monoxide inhalation. They were placed ahead of a 17-year-old girl because they were considered to be more desperately in need of a transplant. During the course of writing the story, the reporter learned that the 17-year-old girl had died.

Was the hospital's decision fair? Is it right to provide liver transplants to patients who have damaged their own liver by drinking alcohol? Should the sickest patients be treated first? Or should doctors be allowed to use their own judgment to help those whom they consider most likely to benefit from transplants?

This is an even tougher question to answer when patients come back for a second or third transplant after earlier operations have failed. The surgeons involved in the early attempts often feel a loyalty to the patient and a commitment to follow through to the bitter end, even though experience shows clearly that the chance of success falls off rapidly if the first transplant fails. In effect, because of their personal relationship, surgeons will give a new heart, kidney, or liver to a patient who is less likely to benefit from it than another person on the waiting list. Should the medical team always help the person nearest death, or should it try to help the person most likely to benefit over the long haul?

These questions, difficult as they are, deal mainly with providing organs to individuals. Even tougher are questions concerning entire segments of society. One question that arose while the U.S. Congress was writing the transplant law in 1984 was: What should be done about foreigners? At the time, several newspapers had published reports of organs being shipped to foreign transplant centers. In reaction, the new law limited the export of organs—no more than 10% of those collected each year can go out of the country. But what if the foreigners can afford to fly to an American transplant center that has easy access to organs? Should organs from U.S. citizens be reserved exclusively for U.S. citizens? There is no rule of this kind, and there are persistent reports that wealthy patients, including wealthy foreigners, get special consideration at some transplant centers.

There are also questions concerning whether medical professionals may favor certain segments of American society over others when deciding who should receive an organ transplant. A recent study by Paul Held of the Urban Institute in Washington, D.C., confirmed what has been found in years past: Whites are more likely to receive kidney transplants than blacks are, men more likely than women.

Although researchers have not pinpointed exactly where bias comes in, it is clear that it does come in at some point in the decision process. Some think the bias may enter when doctors exercise their discretion in deciding who should be put on the waiting list for a transplant. Once a patient is in line, he or she advances toward the operation strictly according to medical need. Steps are being taken now by transplant doctors to reach out to kidney dialysis centers in poor, often black, areas to anticipate need and thus overcome the kind of bias the survey reveals. That white men appear to get better treatment, even though great effort has gone into making the system accessible to all needy patients, shows just how difficult it is to apply broad ethical principles to the practice of medicine.

Some say that the organ transplant program reflects another kind of bias, a bias that favors high technology and high drama

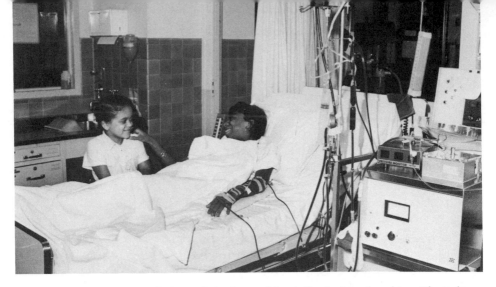

A woman on a kidney dialysis machine talks to her daughter. There is much controversy concerning waiting lists for organ donations; one study has shown that whites are more likely than blacks to receive kidney transplants.

at the expense of a broad program of preventive health care. The media focus on organ transplant cases because they often involve acute life-or-death dilemmas and involve the macabre aspects of high-tech medicine. Perhaps because of this attention, this specialized field has received considerable public support. But some states, such as Oregon, are asking whether it might not be more sensible to limit expenses on organ transplants and allocate more tax dollars for the care of the large number of people—especially children—who otherwise would not get to the doctor's office at all.

This is a tough ethical stance to uphold. Even if it is the right thing to do for society, it is difficult to carry out on an individual basis, for it means in some cases that patients will die sooner as a result. This dilemma is described in the last chapter of this book.

ON THE HORIZON

The great demand for organs and the frustration of working within federal rules have led a few writers to suggest a radical change. They say the United States should move to a *free market* system, in which organs could be bought and sold.

Many decisions on the allocation of goods in the United States are simply left to the operations of the free market for settlement. Doctors and hospitals profit from organ transplantations; why should it be less appropriate for the family of someone who donates an organ to make money? Advocates of this approach concede that there is something "repugnant" about the idea of buying and selling human parts, but they argue that taking this step would quickly increase the number of organs available. Also, it might do away with some of the agonizing dilemmas concerning who should receive organs.

The general view, as expressed by members of the American Society of Transplant Physicians (ASTP), is that this practice would be "ethically indefensible." "It is immoral to offer someone an incentive to undergo permanent physical damage," according to Charles M. Carpenter, Robert B. Ettenger, and Terry B. Strom, members of ASTP. It is "ethically impossible for physicians to justify removal of kidneys from living unrelated persons when we are using only a small fraction of the available cadaveric organs," they conclude. This view is likely to prevail. It is not only federal law; nine states have made laws to this effect.

Technology may offer another way out of the organ-supply crisis. Some doctors have experimented with *xenografting*, which involves transplanting parts from animals to humans. This practice also has its ethically questionable side. Animal rights advocates have served notice that they will block any large-scale effort to cultivate animals simply for "mutilation" in an attempt to sustain human lives. But the main obstacle is that xenografts so far have not had lasting practical success.

The other great hope is that man-made hearts, kidneys, and

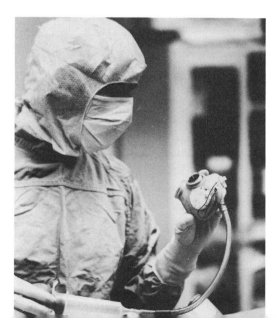

Dr. Robert Jarvik prepares to implant his invention, the Jarvik-7 artificial heart, into William Schroeder's chest in November 1984. Schroeder lived 620 days after the operation, making him the longest-surviving artificial-heart recipient.

livers can be made to serve as permanent replacements for natural organs. Although the medical profession has had success in developing artificial bone and joint replacements, the record is not as good on the complicated internal organs.

Perhaps the best-known experiment in this area was the attempt in 1982 to implant an artificial heart in a 61-year-old dentist named Barney Clark. The operation, performed by surgeon William DeVries, attempted to put a "permanent" mechanical heart made by Robert Jarvik in Clark's chest. The first implant failed in a matter of hours. The second lasted 12 days. The third worked but produced numerous side effects, including blood clotting, seizures, and psychic stress. Clark died after four months, spending most of that time less than fully conscious.

There have been three other attempts to use a full-size Jarvik heart. The last was in 1984, when William Schroeder was given a Jarvik-7 heart. He lived 620 days, 132 days longer than did any other recipient of a permanent artificial heart, but on August 6, 1986, he died of a stroke. Experts believe that the use of permanent artificial hearts will not become common unless a model is designed that does not cause the strokes that killed Schroeder and Murray Haydon, another Jarvik-7 heart recipient.

The FDA and the NIH have decided that the "completely implantable" artificial heart has not emerged from the experimental stage. It is not ready for general use. However, physicians are using a smaller version of the Jarvik heart, one that must be tethered to a large power console, as a "bridge" to a transplant operation. Some patients whose own heart fails are given a Jarvik device temporarily until a transplantable human organ can be found. About 50 such operations have been performed in the United States since Clark's surgery. But because the few other attempts to use the full-size Jarvik devices as permanent replacements for the human heart have failed, research continues on other types of artificial hearts.

There is hope that technical ingenuity may one day do away with the hard ethical questions medicine faces as to who should give and who should be first to receive precious organs. For the foreseeable future, however, these questions will remain.

• • • •

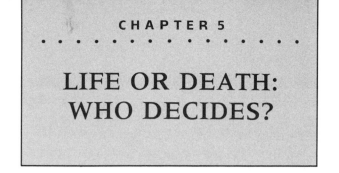

CHAPTER 5

LIFE OR DEATH: WHO DECIDES?

Charles Griffith, who shot his comatose three-year-old daughter, appears in court.

In April 1975, Karen Ann Quinlan drank several gin and tonics at her boyfriend's birthday party, several hours after she had taken a mild tranquilizer. The combination of drugs and alcohol sent the 21 year old into a coma (a state of deep unconsciousness). At the hospital, Quinlan was attached to a respirator, which physicians said was necessary to maintain her breathing.

Quinlan was not the first person to lapse into a coma after mixing alcohol and tranquilizers. But her case marked a turning point in the United States in the debate over patients' rights.

After doctors decided Quinlan's coma was irreversible, her parents requested that the life support equipment be disconnected, even though they knew this would probably lead to her death. This request prompted the nation's medical community and legal system to confront publicly the tough questions related to an individual's right to self-determination, including the choice of death.

In 1976, in a landmark right-to-die case, the New Jersey Supreme Court honored the request from Quinlan's parents to disconnect the respirator. Quinlan did not die immediately; she breathed on her own in an unconscious state for nine years until she died in 1985.

More than 10,000 Americans now "live" in what physicians call a "persistent vegetative state" in hospitals and nursing homes across the country. Although medicine, with its array of advanced technologies and drugs, is able to keep these patients alive longer, ethical questions arise as to whether the preservation of life should take precedence over the relief of suffering and an individual's right to die with dignity.

LIFE-AND-DEATH DECISIONS

The Quinlan case is not the typical example of a dying patient. Most people do not languish for years in a vegetative state, needing help from a person or machine to carry out even the most basic activities of daily living: eating, drinking, bathing, getting to a bathroom. More often, death occurs quickly in hospital *intensive care units* (ICUs). In all these cases, however, ethical dilemmas are troubling and painful to medical personnel, patients, families, and friends. Rapid advances in medical techniques and technologies have enabled patients entering ICUs to survive traumas, such as heart attacks, that routinely killed people in earlier times. But death inevitably involves cardiac arrest, whatever the primary cause of death.

Although doctors do not take lightly decisions about whether to resuscitate an unconscious patient, they must act quickly because once a person's heart stops beating, any delay reduces the effectiveness of the resuscitation effort. Such decisions come up every day in hospitals and other health-care settings across the

Karen Ann Quinlan's parents. In a historic 1976 decision, the New Jersey Supreme Court authorized doctors to honor the Quinlans' request to disconnect the life support system connected to their daughter, who was in an irreversible coma.

country. Each time, medical personnel must consider whether the intrusive, painful, and costly procedures used in resuscitation are likely to succeed and whether they will lead only to a life of prolonged suffering. There are no guarantees. Because a procedure worked before does not ensure that it will prove effective for the next patient.

Do-Not-Resuscitate Orders

Efforts to resuscitate patients are successful in only about one in three attempts. Of those who survive, only one in three has a chance of being discharged from the hospital. Those patients who do return home are often significantly impaired with permanent disabilities, such as paralysis, that they may have suffered before being resuscitated. One might think it always desirable to resuscitate a patient when possible; however this is not a simple question. Many feel it is sometimes better to let the death occur. This has led to the development of do-not-resuscitate orders, which provide a basis for the decision as to when patients should not be resuscitated.

Effective January 1, 1988, a national organization that accredits hospitals required all institutions to establish written DNR policies. The stamp of approval by this body, the Chicago-based Joint Commission on Accreditation of Health Care Organizations, is important because hospitals cannot get any federal funds if they are not accredited. The average hospital earns about 40% of its revenues from treating the elderly and disabled under Medicare. Without those funds, many hospitals could not operate. DNR orders are not given easily, but their existence has become a necessity. Because of the Joint Commission's requirement, an increasing number of providers of health care are drafting DNR policies or reassessing their current policies. As it stands, policies vary greatly among institutions; DNR means different things to different doctors. The Joint Commission does not require specific policy contents. It does require that the policy should describe the mechanism for reaching decisions about withholding patient treatment; describe how conflicts in decision making can be resolved; describe the role of each component of the medical staff and the role of the family members in the decision process; and ensure that patients' rights and desires are considered.

The Bouvia Case

Fortunately, most people who visit physicians and enter hospitals each year are discharged, healthy and able to resume a productive

In state supreme court, Elizabeth Bouvia, a quadriplegic with cerebral palsy, won the right to refuse being force-fed at a California hospital.

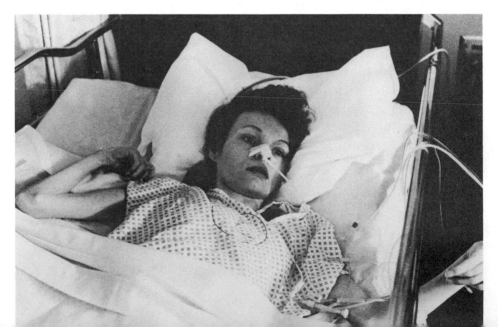

life. DNR decisions do not come into play. But what about the less fortunate, those for whom life becomes degrading?

Consider the case of Elizabeth Bouvia, a victim of cerebral palsy and a quadriplegic since birth, who has virtually no control of her bodily functions or use of her limbs. In 1984, at age 26, Bouvia checked into the medical center at the University of Southern California in Los Angeles.

After four months in the facility, however, she asked that the hospital allow her to starve herself to death, providing only pain-killing drugs and hygienic care to maintain her bodily cleanliness. She said she no longer wished to live with her physical limitations. The hospital refused to honor her request and inserted nasal feeding tubes. The California Superior Court backed the hospital's right to force-feed her even though she had been declared mentally competent. The case sparked a firestorm of debate.

Eventually, the California Supreme Court overruled the lower court's decision, saying that Bouvia "had the fundamental right to refuse medical treatment" on the basis of the constitutional right to privacy, guaranteed by the Fifth Amendment through various Supreme Court decisions. Although Bouvia won her court case, she decided to continue eating and, as of March 1988, was still living at the hospital.

Although in both the Quinlan case and the Bouvia case the courts backed the patients' right to dignified death, ethicists, theologians, physicians, and families continue to wrestle with difficult life-and-death decisions. Even though the courts have set precedents, the choices have become no easier.

PATIENTS' RIGHTS

A 1988 poll taken by the Graduate School of Public Affairs at the University of Colorado at Denver found that 81% of the survey's respondents wanted "expected quality of life" to be considered when deciding whether one should be treated with critical-care technology. Sixty-two percent of those answering the survey said they would rather die than live out their life on a respirator.

Responding to a survey, however, is different from actually making a hard choice about intrusive medical care. What one wants in theory and what one wants when faced with a life-and-death situation can be worlds apart. Part of the difficulty is that there are no hard-and-fast rules.

Informing the Patient

Ethicists and medical practitioners now generally seem to agree on broad-based principles to guide DNR policies and decisions on life-prolonging treatment. Medical experts agree that the patient's wishes should, whenever possible, direct the course of treatment. Information, however, is crucial to making those choices.

Thus, they also feel that physicians and other health-care professionals have a responsibility to take time to discuss options that are open to the patient; that patients should rarely, if ever, be kept from hearing the truth; and that patients should have the opportunity to make informed choices. That means dying patients should be given as much information as they wish about the nature of the disease and the prognosis. Such information should be given as early in the treatment as possible, and medical ethicists also argue that doctors should fully inform all patients about the range of treatment options from which they can choose.

Curiously, the United States appears to differ from many other industrialized countries over the issue of how much information a terminally ill patient should be given about his or her condition. In Japan, for example, a recent survey of physicians revealed that fewer than 20% of doctors tell patients of a diagnosis of cancer. Traditionally, they feel that the depression resulting from the truth is physically detrimental. This tradition was demonstrated in the case of Emperor Hirohito, who became seriously ill with cancer in September 1988 but was never informed of the diagnosis before his death on January 7, 1989. The results of the Japanese study are similar to findings of a poll published by the American Medical Association (AMA) in 1961, revealing that only 12% of U.S. physicians thought patients should be told they had terminal cancer. By 1979, however, the *Journal of the American Medical Association* reported that virtually all American physicians agreed on the need to tell their patients the truth.

Besides the right to information, medical ethicists appear to agree that a mentally competent patient with either a terminal

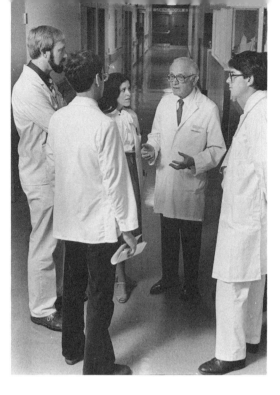

When people are seriously injured but have not left a living will or designated a surrogate, doctors, as well as family members, must often make difficult decisions.

or nonterminal condition has the right to order the withholding or withdrawal of lifesaving or life-prolonging treatment. At times, that decision may conflict with what medical professionals perceive as their primary responsibility—to save lives.

Patients have the right to determine the course of their own treatment if their decision is well informed, sound, and does not infringe on the rights of others. But is it a "sound," competent decision if a patient bases a life-sustaining decision on a religious belief? Some people refuse treatment because they interpret their physical pain and suffering as a sign of punishment for some sin they have committed. Hindus view their present suffering as a consequence of transgressions in an earlier lifetime. Jehovah's Witnesses, a fundamentalist Christian group with more than 3 million members worldwide, believe that the Old Testament prohibits them from taking blood into the body by any route. Medical dilemmas arise, therefore, when physicians confront a situation in which they could save the life of a Jehovah's Witness through a blood transfusion, but the patient refuses to allow for such treatment.

Is that patient making a competent decision, for example, if refusing such treatment will lead to certain death and leave a family of three children without a mother or father? Should the family be allowed to overrule the wishes of the patient? Should parents be allowed to make such medical decisions for their children, based on religious beliefs, if those decisions will lead to death? Although some courts have ruled that parents have no right to endanger their child's health in following their religious beliefs, most state legislatures have enacted laws accommodating spiritual healing, or the use of nonmedical, often religious methods of healing. In most of these laws, adults are allowed to choose methods of spiritual healing for themselves unless they are the sole surviving parent of a child and the method might endanger their life; they are not allowed to make choices that may endanger their child.

Questions of religion aside, it is important that medical personnel determine whether a patient's choice to reject life-sustaining treatment is merely a request for relief from pain, which can often be done by less drastic means such as administering stronger medication.

Many times, doctors must try to understand whether the request to unplug life-sustaining equipment reflects a desire to relieve family members of the perceived burden of watching over and caring for the patient. Direct, candid discussion among all the parties involved can help alleviate some of that anxiety. In addition, relief from physical pain is available in most instances.

Surrogates and Living Wills

Making treatment decisions when one is in pain or in a life-threatening situation can be enormously stressful. Consequently, medical experts urge patients to make their views and wishes about such situations known to both their personal physician and family long they before have to confront such decisions.

This is best done through the use of advance directives. For example, one can confer binding legal power for medical decisions on a *surrogate*, a person appointed in advance to speak for someone if he or she is unable to do so. The surrogate must faithfully carry out the wishes of the patient. If the patient fails to make such wishes known, then the surrogate must consider the values of the individual and what a "reasonable" person would wish in the same situation.

Making such critical decisions for another person, however, can cause guilt and pain. To ease that situation and to relieve family, friends, and physicians of the agony of a surrogate decision made without clear instructions, an increasing number of people are making their wishes known through *living wills*. In most states, these are legally binding documents that allow an individual to lay down specific directions regarding treatment or refusal of treatment during a terminal illness. When drafting such a document, however, individuals must distinguish between specific life-prolonging and lifesaving procedures that might be performed on them. For example, they might choose not to be placed on a respirator but might still ask that, if necessary, resuscitation procedures be conducted.

The use of living wills and surrogates can be an effective means of helping to ensure that an individual's desires about medical care are fulfilled. But because such directives are governed by state law, they are often subject to restrictive language. For example, it is common for state laws to restrict advance directives to situations in which the person is "terminally ill," often meaning the last six months of a person's life. But it is difficult for physicians to predict accurately how many months a person has left to live.

Such problems lead many medical ethicists to conclude that advance directives are no substitute for an ongoing, candid, compassionate relationship between patient and physician. Such a relationship becomes especially important when patients have failed to designate a surrogate or to notify family members of their wishes as to the withdrawal of care. For the competent patient, the physician must determine the patient's preferences through informed consent. If, as the result of an illness, the patient is incompetent, the physician may act based upon his or her knowledge of the patient's wishes before the individual became ill.

Even when the patient, physicians, and family agree on treatment, however, the patient's wishes are not always carried out. In mid-June 1987, 27-year-old Angela Carder suddenly had a second bout with cancer. After two years in remission, the disease reappeared, this time in a form that was to prove fatal. In that respect, Carder was like tens of thousands of other Americans annually. But unlike most of those others, Carder was six months pregnant when her cancer resurfaced.

When Carder entered the George Washington University Hospital in Washington, D.C., her physicians found a tumor on her lung and told her she would die within weeks. If she could hold out for at least another three weeks, her fetus would stand a much better chance of surviving, even if she did not. But within days of their diagnosis, the physicians returned to Carder to tell her she might die much sooner.

Carder agreed to take medications to help her survive longer and to soothe her pain. She insisted that treatment decisions be driven by the need to keep her comfortable before taking into account the needs of her fetus. Carder's husband and her physicians agreed to follow her directions, and they informed the hospital administrator of Carder's decision.

But the hospital, fearing a medical malpractice suit, sought a decision from the District of Columbia Superior Court as to what, if anything, should be done with regard to the fetus Carder was carrying. The judge ordered an emergency cesarean section, over the objections of Carder, her family, and her physicians.

Carder's premature baby girl died the same night she was delivered. Carder herself died two days later, in part from complications brought on by the operation itself.

The family was incensed and appealed the court's decision. Although it was too late for Angela Carder, they thought other women should not be placed in a situation in which a court could balance their welfare against that of an unborn child. As for the hospital, its attorney said only that "there were two lives in the balance, and the hospital tried to do the right thing." As of September 1989, the Carder appeal was still pending before the District of Columbia Court of Appeals.

There are other cases to consider: What happens if the patient is no longer competent and has given no informed consent and provided no guidance regarding resuscitation? The situation of the mute patient can be further complicated when the attending physician and the patient's family disagree over the course of treatment. Should the patient be assigned a different physician whose views conform with those of the family?

Hospices

The explicit policies governing DNR orders being compiled by an increasing number of nursing homes and hospitals help answer several questions and bring a sense of order to many split-second medical decisions about whether to resuscitate patients—many of whom have not voiced their wishes on critical care. Thousands of other Americans facing death, however, have made their wishes known by opting for care in nontraditional settings.

These patients have chosen to spend their final days in a hospice. The goals of hospice care are to minimize the patient's pain and to control disease symptoms without using heroic, lifesaving measures.

During medieval times, hospices were comfort stations for crusaders. It was not until the late 19th century that they came to be known as places in which Roman Catholic nuns cared for the dying.

The modern hospice movement, begun in England in the 1960s, was founded on the idea of applying modern medical techniques to control the pain of the terminally ill. Rather than focus on traditional acute medical-care procedures, hospices give

Married nearly 50 years, this couple chose to spend their last years together at home receiving hospice care, which minimizes pain and keeps patients comfortable without using heroic measures.

supportive and palliative care, or care to reduce pain and suffering most often in the patient's home or in homelike settings. The patient's family is considered an integral part of the effort to provide care. The family is involved in treatment decisions and encouraged to prepare for the patient's death.

There are currently about 2,000 hospices in the United States, and an increasing percentage of those facilities are treating patients with AIDS. In addition to providing care, they provide an environment in which patients can die peacefully and with dignity, an alternative many favor to impersonal, institutional settings.

Refusing Treatment

Some patients choose to spend their final days in a hospice and allow nature to relieve them of their suffering; other patients can die only by refusing medical treatment or nutrition. Despite guidelines spelling out the right to refuse treatment, patients' wishes are sometimes ignored. A 1987 report from the Office of Technology Assessment cited the case of an 82-year-old woman who was attached to a respirator after coronary bypass surgery. "She could not talk because of the tubes in her throat but wrote notes to her daughter, saying, 'Please let me die.' The tubes were not removed, and when she tried to pull them out herself, her hands were strapped to the bed."

A landmark case in 1986 in the Massachusetts Supreme Judicial Court held that a feeding tube could be removed from a patient in a persistent vegetative state if this action were consistent with the patient's previously expressed wishes. But physicians are often hesitant to comply with the wishes of a patient because court rulings nationwide are inconsistent. Although the consensus is that patients should have final say over treatment in almost all cases, some courts have upheld the force-feeding of patients. In the majority of cases involving patients in psychiatric institutions, the nation's courts have ruled that doctors can legally force a patient to take drugs even if the patient objects. The doctor must obtain a court order, however, in order to overrule a patient's objections.

The confusion about treatment decisions also stems from legal cases such as one in 1982 in which Neil L. Barber and Robert J.

Nejdl, two California physicians who agreed to a family's request to remove life support treatment from a hopelessly brain-damaged patient, were charged with murder. After several hearings, the doctors were acquitted by the California Court of Appeals on October 12, 1983. The court ultimately ruled that omitting treatment such as intravenous feeding was justified if the benefit of continuing treatments was outweighed by the burden it imposed on the patient. For the first time, a U.S. court used "quality of life" as a criterion in determining a patient's best interests.

Although state courts have decided many right-to-die cases, the Supreme Court first agreed to hear one during the 1989–90 session. The case, *Cruzan v. Harmon*, involved Nancy Beth Cruzan—an unconscious brain-injured woman whose parents requested the removal of the feeding tube that maintains her. The Missouri Supreme Court's decision was that the state's "unqualified interest in life" overrode the wishes of the patient and her family. Whatever the Supreme Court's decision on this case may be, it will have a far-reaching effect with implications for many related right-to-privacy issues.

Physicians and families faced tough court battles in several other important bioethics cases in the early 1980s. Medical ethicists stress the importance of effective communication in patient-physician relationships and the need for patients, in most cases, to control the course of treatment. But what happens when the rights of a newborn are involved? Should parents have final say over a course of treatment?

One case that drew national attention was that of Baby Doe, who was born in 1982 in Bloomington, Indiana. Baby Doe was born with *Down's syndrome* (a chromosome disorder that causes mental retardation and a set of specific physical abnormalities) and a defective esophagus. The parents decided to deny the child food and corrective surgery. An Indiana court upheld the parents' decision, and the child died after living six days. A month later, the federal government waded into the controversy, stating that hospitals receiving federal money could not withhold care from a handicapped infant. To help police that action, the federal government placed posters in hospital nurseries spelling out the new decree and set up a 24-hour telephone hot line for people to call if they suspected wrongdoing.

In the ensuing months, several other well-publicized cases of parents refusing medical care for their infants born with debilitating, life-shortening medical problems fueled the debate. In June 1986, the U.S. Supreme Court finally ruled on *American Hospital Association v. Otis Bowen*: The federal government was to have no role in regulating the delivery of care in hospital nurseries. State governments were to have sole jurisdiction.

Although the Supreme Court has ruled on the matter, the debate continues. If a decision about medical care is taken from the hands of parents and physicians, does the government also become responsible for supporting the patient through the remainder of his or her life? Whereas one side in the debate calls for safeguards for the newborn handicapped, the opposing side questions the humaneness of saddling parents with the serious burden of caring for the severely disabled child without providing substantive financial help.

Euthanasia

Although withdrawing life-supporting treatment raises complex questions of medical ethics, vexing problems also appear in the debate over *active euthanasia*. The word *euthanasia* comes from two Greek words that mean "good" and "death." In more recent times, people have equated euthanasia with the term *mercy killing*. Euthanasia can mean allowing death to take its course without intervening or permitting it to occur through withdrawal of life support. Active euthanasia, as the term implies, is more likely to mean giving a terminally ill patient a fatal injection.

A 1987 public opinion poll by Louis Harris and Associates found that more than half of the respondents said it was appropriate for doctors to help terminally ill patients die, if the patients request it. But the survey revealed markedly different results among doctors and nurses. About two-thirds of the doctors and almost three-fifths of the nurses interviewed said they felt that euthanasia was wrong.

A more recent poll showed that of 509 lawyers surveyed in 1988, more than half said they believe the administration of lethal injections to terminally ill patients should be legal. The AMA, which represents almost 250,000 doctors in the United States, disagrees. The AMA holds that "for humane reasons, and with informed consent," a doctor may "cease or omit treatment" to a terminally ill patient, allowing the person to die. But the association rejects the idea of active euthanasia. A doctor "should not intentionally cause death," the AMA's ethics council declared in 1986 and reaffirmed in 1988.

Despite the opposition of physicians and religious groups to voluntary, or active, euthanasia, supporters of the concept were almost successful in putting the issue before California voters in 1988. The Los Angeles–based Hemlock Society argues that dying patients should be able to ask their doctor to help them die. The society proposed that California legalize patients' euthanasia requests. The law would have applied only to terminally ill patients in the last six months of life, as certified by two doctors.

The California initiative was fashioned after medical practice in the Netherlands. Although active euthanasia is officially illegal there, it is tolerated in almost all circumstances if physicians follow strict, but sometimes contradictory, guidelines. It is all right to assist in a suicide if the terminally ill person wishes to die, is suffering, has asked to die over a period of time, is physically unable to commit euthanasia unassisted, and the doctor and one other person have approved of it. Even if all these conditions are met, the assisted suicide is not permitted if it would cause "unnecessary suffering" to others. In 1985, the California State Commission on Euthanasia published a study concluding that assisted euthanasia was illegal except in a "medical emergency," which was defined as existing "if continued life would only distort a patient's personality and aggravate the suffering" and "if the patient would not otherwise be able to die with dignity worthy of a human being." The vagueness of the terms *unnecessary suffering* and *medical emergency* make these guidelines less than black and white, ensuring that even in the Netherlands, where active euthanasia accounts for as many as 7,000 deaths annually, there is still much debate about the issue.

The heart of the controversy in the Netherlands and the United States centers on whether legalizing active euthanasia will lead to abuse. Opponents of the practice worry that once active euthanasia is legal, society will tumble down a "slippery slope" in which criteria for who can request assistance in dying are relaxed. Society might use the procedure to rid itself of undesirables. The haunting memories of Nazi Germany and its World War II death camps still cast long shadows. Proponents of voluntary euthanasia also acknowledge the need to guard against the "mercy killing" of the mentally impaired, physically handicapped, and other people tagged by some as "undesirables." They call for tightly regulated safeguards to protect patients.

Opponents of active euthanasia also argue that legalizing it will undermine the fragile and important element of trust in patient-physician relationships, especially for those in nursing homes. Opponents worry that frail and weakened patients could succumb to suggestions from physicians or even family members that they ask for a lethal injection.

Opponents of active euthanasia used a January 1988 article printed in the *Journal of the American Medical Association* as support for their concern. The author, an anonymous physician, claimed he injected a fatal dose of morphine into a 20-year-old woman dying of ovarian cancer. In the four-paragraph essay, entitled "It's Over, Debbie," the author wrote: "The room seemed filled with the patient's desperate effort to survive. . . . It was a gallows scene, a cruel mockery of her youth and unfulfilled potential. Her only words to me were, 'Let's get this over with'."

Response to the article from the medical community and medical ethicists was swift and tempestuous. The young physician was largely denounced for killing the patient but even more so for killing a patient whom he had never seen before and about whose medical history he knew almost nothing. The furor also touched off a national debate about euthanasia.

But advocates see the issue as one of patients' rights. They point out that because patients are now allowed to terminate life support treatment, including food and water, it is logical and humane to allow patients to decide when they wish to die. Is it humane and dignified, advocates ask, to allow a patient to die slowly and in pain? Moreover, they add, physicians who object to helping patients die can simply decline to help.

Questions about euthanasia and the broader issues of life-sustaining and lifesaving medical interventions are certain to multiply. As society continues pouring millions of dollars into advancing medical science aimed at extending life, it is also increasing the complexity of death. And, at the same time that medical science discovers more and more about sustaining life, people may become less and less able to afford applying this knowledge on a broad scale for all members of society.

•   •   •   •

CHAPTER 6

ALLOCATION
OF SCARCE
RESOURCES

After personal pleas on television and in newspapers nation-wide, seven-year-old Coby Howard, who suffered from acute lymphocytic leukemia, had more than half of the money he needed for a bone marrow transplant that might save his life. Two months after the campaign for funds began, however, Coby's family had raised only three-fourths of the money required by the transplantation facility. Before the remainder could be collected, the boy died.

Ironically, had young Coby Howard been in line for the operation only 12 months earlier, the state in which he lived would have paid for the cost of the operation and the necessary and expensive follow-up care.

Was the boy's death unnecessary? Should he have been spared having to perform publicly in an effort to raise the needed funds, or was the seven year old merely another victim of an increasingly widespread and often deadly game of choices being played across the United States?

Consider the options a state lawmaker might have and the choices he or she might have to make. Money is tight for the state's program of providing health care to low-income residents. Over the past several years the state has covered those in need of bone marrow, heart, liver, and pancreas transplants, but the program has met with mixed success. Without the operations, the people would surely die. Even with the operations, however, there are no guarantees of success. Past records show that from 1985 to 1987, for example, the state funded 19 transplantations at a cost of $1 million, yet only 9 of the patients survived. And for those who survived, the total annual cost of follow-up care was about $225,000.

A lawmaker might have to vote on whether to continue allocating a minimum of about $1 million during the next 2 years to continue the transplant program or to use those same funds and extend health-care coverage to about 1,500 previously uncovered pregnant women and children of low-income households.

The lawmaker would know that the incidence of low birth weight babies is significantly higher among low-income women than among more affluent women and that low birth weight infants are more likely to be victims of infant mortality. The lawmaker would know that repeated studies have shown that for every dollar spent on prenatal care, the state saved about three dollars in expenses for postnatal care during the first year of life, required primarily for low birth weight babies. He or she would also know that, largely as a result of insufficient prenatal care, 1 in 10 U.S. babies dies before reaching his or her first birthday and that the United States ranks 19th among industrialized nations in infant mortality. Although the lawmaker's situation as stated here is hypothetical, it is similar to ones faced every day in many states.

In June 1987, 75 lawmakers in the state of Oregon made their choice. For the news media and the public at large, the legislators

Infant Mortality Rates

Infant deaths per 1,000 live births in 20 industrialized countries*

United States	10.3		Canada	7.9

Austria	9.9		Norway	7.8

Belgium	9.7		Hong Kong	7.7

United Kingdom	9.1		France	7.6

Australia	8.7		Netherlands	7.6

Ireland	8.7		Singapore	7.4

Federal Republic of Germany	8.6		Switzerland	6.8

German Democratic Republic	8.5		Finland	5.8

Spain	8.5		Sweden	5.7

Denmark	8.2		Japan	5.2

*Rates are the number of deaths of infants under 1 year of age per 1,000 live births. Data exclude fetal deaths.
Note: Figures are the latest available from each country for the years 1985, 1986, and 1987.
Source: United Nations Department of International Economic and Social Affairs, Statistical Office

were ultimately seen as playing God and deciding who should live and who should die. Their vote to discontinue Oregon's organ transplantation program sparked a national hue and cry when in November of that year the state denied funding for Coby Howard's bone marrow transplant.

Although the Oregon experience struck an alarming chord for perhaps hundreds of thousands of Americans nationwide, the actions of the 75 lawmakers only highlighted what are increasingly more frequent and explicit decisions about who gets what care, who decides, and on what basis the decisions are made.

One legislator said of the vote, "We all hate it, but we can't walk away from this issue any more. It goes way beyond transplants. How can we spend every nickel in support of a few people when thousands never see a doctor or eat a decent meal?" Oregon lawmakers are not the only state legislators limiting their public financing of organ transplants, and they are not alone in the dilemma of how to allocate scarce public resources. In the wake of the Oregon legislature's decision, one medical ethicist said, "The public has yet to realize that choices must be made and priorities set."

Explicit decisions about providing care to one group of people at the expense of another group capture the imagination of the public at large, especially in cases of organ transplants. One leading medical ethicist said, "The public is fascinated by high technology and particularly organ transplants. Taking parts from dead bodies and putting them into live bodies is fascinating, macabre, strange, and thought-provoking."

In addition, there are only a limited number of organs available for transplantation, an issue that raises complex and often perplexing questions. Should ability to pay for such organ transplants or the age of the potential recipient drive allocation decisions? Who should make these decisions?

THE COST OF CARE

Although organ transplantation presents clear issues for debate and discussion, other decisions regarding rationing of care are less sharply defined. Providers of health care make life-and-death decisions daily as to how aggressively to treat an array of conditions for a wide range of patients. Those decisions are not so visible, not so public. A seemingly endless variety of procedures and drugs is available. Physicians and other health-care professionals make decisions to limit the amount of care they give based on a complex set of variables, including the wishes of the patient, the condition and prognosis of the patient, and, at times, the relative worth of the benefit to the patient versus the additional expense.

There are still other decisions, made neither by lawmakers nor physicians, that in some ways have more profound influence on the kind of care that patients receive and how aggressively they are treated. Pricing decisions by manufacturers of pharmaceuticals and advanced medical technologies can have a powerful effect on the use of emerging treatments.

For example, people with *hemophilia* (an inherited disorder in which one's blood lacks a certain factor necessary for clotting) are likely candidates for blood transfusions, and with the spread of AIDS in society, they are increasingly concerned about the safety of the nation's blood supply. The two most common types of hemophilia are hemophilia A, in which one lacks factor VIII; and hemophilia B, in which factor IX is missing. Hemophiliacs are given transfusions of concentrated blood products, containing large amounts of the missing factor. A transfusion from an individual who is not a hemophiliac, therefore, provides the needed factor but also poses the risk that one of the blood donors might have AIDS.

All hospitals now test donated blood for HIV to lessen this risk. But, unfortunately, by 1989 more than 600 people with hemophilia had contracted AIDS from such transfusions. To lessen their need for transfusions, hemophiliacs have sought an effective blood-clotting treatment. Science has finally met that need, but the price per individual is high: $25,000 annually, about 5 to 8 times the cost of the conventional clotting treatment. Despite

Ryan White, who contracted AIDS through treatment for his hemophilia, listens to his teacher and classmates over a special telephone hook-up. After being diagnosed, White was not allowed to attend school.

the cost, the new, more effective synthetic factor is expected soon to become the standard treatment.

Given hemophiliacs' desperate need for a highly effective blood-clotting agent, does the pharmaceutical company have an ethical obligation to reduce the cost, particularly for lower-income or uninsured hemophiliacs who may be unable to afford it?

When one thinks of choice in the delivery of health-care services, one traditionally thinks of the variety of drugs available and options for life-prolonging or even lifesaving treatments. But the cost of that treatment is increasingly a powerful variable being factored into health-care decisions—not simply by physicians but also by health insurers and lawmakers. Because the vast majority of Americans are covered by public or private health insurance, decisions by legislators affecting public health-care protection and by insurers for those covered under private plans may determine the type of care Americans receive.

In fact, because the costs of the new treatments and health-care services are exploding, public and private insurance programs are trying to constrain growth in the health-care dollars they spend. In public programs, such as the one in Oregon, that often means reducing the scope of covered services and the number of people eligible for care. In private programs, insurers may simply raise the *deductible* (the amount of money that the insured person must pay before the insurance company begins to cover expenses) to discourage people from seeking care unnecessarily.

The combination of actions, however, results in an increasing number of Americans being unable to afford private insurance and yet not qualifying for public programs. By 1988, more than 37 million Americans—1 in 6—had no health insurance; almost half of the uninsured were children under age 13, even though often one of their parents worked. In addition, up to 50 million more people had insufficient insurance coverage to meet their health-care needs, according to a 1987 estimate from the Urban Institute.

Some health economists predict the number of uninsured people could jump to 50 million by the turn of the century, especially in light of the inability of individuals with AIDS-related conditions to obtain affordable insurance. More than 100,000 AIDS cases in the United States were reported to the Centers for Disease

Control (CDC) by mid-January 1989—a number that could jump to 365,000 by 1992, the CDC estimates.

The United States is the only industrialized country in the world that does not provide health-care coverage in the form of either insurance or services for all of its citizens, regardless of ability to pay. Ironically, America spends more on health care per person than any other country in the world—about $2,000 per person annually by 1988. And the expenses are rising.

In large part, the greater cost of health care in the United States and the higher per capita outlay for health-care services reflect the use of more advanced medical technologies. Although virtually all those without health insurance ultimately receive some care, not all Americans receive the same level of care.

Bruce Vladeck, president of the United Hospital Fund, recently said, "The poor can no longer expect the same standard of care as the middle class." To bolster his argument, he noted that patients without health insurance at a New York public hospital will be moved to large wards with up to 20 beds within 2 days after surgery. "They'd better hope that a family member shows up to assist in nursing," he added.

Even when patients have insurance, however, the level of payment for medical services can influence physician care. One cardiologist at a small southern hospital once admitted that his facility had a "silent policy" of not giving an extremely helpful—but very expensive—drug to low-income and elderly heart attack victims because the government payment to the hospital for treating such cases was small. Instead, those patients received a somewhat less effective treatment costing one-tenth as much.

In the mid-1980s, hospitals faced repeated, though largely unsubstantiated, charges of denying care to patients without health insurance or giving them only minimal service before turning them out of the emergency rooms. In response, hospitals said that although the care may have been minimal, it was sufficient. Hospital emergency rooms have a responsibility to provide emergency care to all those in need of it. Providing a full range of services to all patients who come to the door, regardless of the ability to pay, they said, would ultimately cripple the hospitals financially. And closing hospitals would ultimately hurt the needy.

Ironically, although numerous national polls show that the

101

Although polls show that Americans think everyone should have access to the same quality of medical care, few are willing to pay for the care of those who cannot afford it. Children make up an increasing percentage of those below the poverty line in the United States and account for more than half of those without insurance.

majority of Americans overwhelmingly agree that all their fellow citizens—rich or poor—should have access to the same quality of health care, the same surveys indicate that very few Americans would be willing to pay for care for those who cannot afford it.

For medical ethicists and providers of health care, the question of how much care is appropriate is usually driven by considerations of cost. Should costs enter into considerations of who gets care and how much care they get? In an ideal world, perhaps it would not.

HARD CHOICES

Medical ethicists and even most providers of health care now concede that the question is no longer whether health care needs to be rationed. Instead, the question is how to ration it in a just and equitable manner.

Still, some health economists and medical ethicists argue that before trying to make decisions about who should get care when resources are limited, the country must first determine whether the care it is now receiving is necessary. Although medical breakthroughs seem to occur with stunning regularity, insurers and physicians are now asking whether the new technology or medicine is worth the extra dollars. Because public and private insurers foot the bulk of the bill for such new services, they are casting a critical eye on such advances and asking whether the country can afford them, even if they save a few lives.

Expensive Technology

The medical community seems to have a special fascination with new multimillion-dollar technologies, such as positron emission tomography—a diagnostic imaging machine capable of detecting *metabolic* (chemical growth and repair) activity in the heart muscle, for example, without having the patient undergo surgery.

Although such a procedure is generally safer for patients and represents a scientific advance, can the United States afford the $2 million to $3 million price tag? Most hospitals now have CAT scanners. Even so, CAT scanners, first introduced in the early 1970s, are less sophisticated and informative than are newer imaging devices. But some medical ethicists and health economists argue that spending more on newer devices shortchanges expenditures on basic health-care coverage for more Americans.

Sometimes the problem is not that the cost to treat each individual patient with new technologies is too high. In fact, many highly effective services are less expensive than the old technologies. But because these new devices are often safer than the technologies they have replaced, medical barriers limiting their use have been lifted. That means more people have access to the service, thus raising overall health costs.

Is it acceptable to contain costs by stifling the development of new technologies? Probably not, say physicians and medical ethicists. However, attempts to answer such questions definitively are clouded by efforts to balance individual and societal needs. Indeed, most people want the best medical care for themselves and their loved ones. If a new device helps physicians diagnose and treat them better than do other technologies, it is worth the price. But some ethicists also note that spending so much money to develop new technologies diverts resources from preventive health-care programs, which are relatively inexpensive yet contribute significantly by catching health problems early.

Health Costs for the Elderly

Leaving aside the question of efficacy, the most heated discussions of rationing concern who should get the limited resources.

Because public health-care expenditures tend to go to the poor, the disabled, and the elderly, ethicists focus attention on those groups and their rightful place in the consumption of limited public dollars.

In March 1984, Colorado governor Richard Lamm ignited a firestorm of protest when he told a group of health lawyers, "We've got a duty to die and get out of the way with all of our machines and artificial hearts and everything else like that and let the other society, our kids, build a reasonable life." Lamm's remark was widely interpreted to mean that the elderly had a duty to "die and get out of the way." Virtually overnight, the governor was catapulted to the forefront of the debate over allocating health-care resources in the United States.

More recently, Daniel Callahan, director of the Hastings Center, a national center for the study of biomedical ethics, invited similar protest when he wrote that soon after the start of the 21st century, the United States will have to limit public health-care services for the elderly. "We will probably have to limit it by setting a specific age limit (late seventies or early eighties) for expensive, life-extending medical care." Much of the debate about allocating scarce resources focuses on the elderly because their numbers are increasing dramatically, their medical care is expensive, and much of that care is provided during the last year of life.

By the year 2010, the percentage of the nation's population age 65 and older is expected to double. That fact sounds an alarm because in 1988, even though those over age 65 composed only 12% of the population, the federal government spent 30% of its overall health-care budget on programs benefiting the elderly. Medicare spent more than $80 billion on the elderly in 1988; that figure is predicted to jump to almost $200 billion by the year 2000.

That about one-third of those health dollars are spent on care during the last year of life, mostly during the last month, alarms health economists and ethicists, perhaps even more than the figure itself does. Callahan and many other ethicists argue that there are better ways to spend money than extending the final weeks of life. They argue that expensive and prolonged treatment of the elderly deprives other groups of younger people of needed health care; those same health-care dollars could be spent on an array of needed social programs.

Advocates for the elderly argue that the dollars spent on medical care, even during the final days of life, are justified. They reject Callahan's idea of setting age thresholds beyond which certain types of care will be withheld. In addition, they question how one can justify stopping "aggressive" medical treatments to save the life of an elderly person when the definition of *aggressive* is relative and subjective.

The debate is likely to intensify in the coming years as the number of elderly grows rapidly and the cost of providing care escalates. Morris B. Abram, former chairman of the President's Commission for the Study of Ethical Problems in Medicine, once summed up the questions facing those engaged in that debate: "For every illness, there is some procedure that can delay the moment of death. The question is: for how long, at what cost, at what pain, at what suffering?"

Situations to Consider

While the United States continues to agonize over such questions, several other countries have already addressed the tough choices more directly. In England, for example, people with arthritis who rely on the British National Health Service often wait, disabled, for five years to receive artificial hips. Dialysis treatments are denied to kidney patients over age 55 in Britain. This may seem harsh to some, but choices had to be made.

In the United States, ethical considerations of who should get care often center on the habits and style of life of the individual. For example, should heavy smokers or drinkers be given the same priority for receiving scarce health resources as nonsmokers and individuals who follow preventive health-care programs?

AIDS Costs

The current AIDS epidemic has generated enormous controversy because in the United States most of the victims of the deadly virus during the 1980s have been male homosexuals and intravenous drug users—two groups long ostracized by the public.

Medicaid pays for 25% of total national AIDS costs. Federal and state governments generally contribute equal shares to Medicaid. In 1989, the states' share of caring for victims of AIDS is projected to top $123 million, up from $10 million only 4 years earlier.

Partly as a consequence of those expenditures, health benefits to other low-income recipients, often pregnant women and dependent children, have been curtailed. That trade-off has led some members of the U.S. Congress to question whether even limited public funds should be spent to care for AIDS victims.

Public Awareness and Participation

In addition to the tough ethical situation presented by AIDS, governments at all levels as well as ordinary citizens also have to face an increasingly complex array of other ethical decisions. Already some communities and states have taken steps to broaden public awareness of the issues involved in such decisions and to solicit public participation in making the hard choices.

By 1989, a dozen states had established grass-roots groups for this purpose. The first such group, begun in Oregon in 1983, trained scores of community leaders around the state, who in turn led discussions with other members of local civic, religious, and political organizations. The Oregon model has been imitated in other states in an effort to develop a community consensus on life-and-death bioethical questions and on how state residents want their tax dollars spent on health care.

There have been questions of medical ethics since ancient times and, no doubt, as long as people live and die, there will continue to be such questions. The acceleration of technological advances in the 20th century has increased the number of ethical problems as well as presenting them at such a rate that it is difficult to keep abreast of the knowledge needed to make intelligent choices in these matters. But at the same time, these advances have provided a choice in situations where there was previously no choice or hope. However, despite wider citizen involvement, the choices will become no simpler. But in the future, the ethical and economic choices may no longer rest solely with legislators, physicians, lawyers, and medical ethicists.

●   ●   ●   ●

APPENDIX:
FOR MORE INFORMATION

The following is a list of national associations and organizations that can provide further information on medical issues of ethical concern.

GENERAL

American Civil Liberties Union
132 West 43rd Street
New York, NY 10016
(212) 944-9800

Office of Disease Prevention and
  Health Promotion
National Health Information Center
P.O. Box 1123
Washington, DC 20013
(800) 336-4797
(301) 565-4167

World Health Organization
Publications Office
49 Sheridan Avenue
Albany, NY 12210
(518) 436-9686

BIOETHICS RESEARCH
INSTITUTIONS

UNITED STATES

American Hospital Association
Special Committee on Biomedical
  Ethics
840 North Lake Shore Drive
Chicago, IL 60611
Paul B. Hofmann, Chairman
(312) 280-6000

American Medical Student
  Association
Standing Committee on Bioethics
1910 Association Drive
Reston, VA 22091
(703) 620-6600

Bioethics Consultation Group
1400 Shattuck Avenue
Suite 6
P.O. Box 10145
Berkeley, CA 94709
(415) 486-0626

Bioethics Institute at St. Francis
  Hospital
250 West 63rd Street
Miami Beach, FL 33141
(305) 868-5000

Castello Institute of Stafford
P.O. Box 279
Stafford, VA 22554
(703) 659-4171

Center for Applied Biomedical
  Ethics
Rose Medical Center
4567 East Ninth Avenue
Denver, CO 80220
(303) 320-2121

Center for Bioethics
St. Joseph Health System
440 South Batavia Street
Orange, CA 92668
(714) 997-7690

Center for Biomedical Ethics
Office of Community Health
Case Western Reserve University
School of Medicine
2119 Abington Road
Cleveland, OH 44106
(216) 368-6196

Center for Biomedical Ethics
University of Minnesota
UMHC Box 33
Harvard Street at East River Road
Minneapolis, MN 55455
(612) 625-4917

Center for Clinical and Research
   Ethics
Vanderbilt University Medical
   Center
Nashville, TN 37232
(615) 322-2252

Center for Ethics and Humanities
   in the Life Sciences
C-208 East Fee Hall
Michigan State University
East Lansing, MI 48824
(517) 355-7550

Center for Ethics, Medicine, and
   Public Issues
Baylor College of Medicine
1200 Moursund Avenue
Houston, TX 77030
(713) 798-6290

Center for Health Ethics and Policy
Graduate School of Public Affairs
University of Colorado at Denver
1200 Larimer Street
Campus Box 133
Denver, CO 80204
(303) 556-4837

Citizens Committee on Biomedical
   Ethics
24 Beechwood Road
P.O. Box 1286
Summit, NJ 07901
(201) 277-3858

The Hastings Center
Institute of Society, Ethics, and the
   Life Sciences, Inc.
255 Elm Road
Briarcliff Manor, NY 10510
(914) 762-8500

Institute for Applied Ethics in
   Reproductive Health
1 West Campbell Avenue
Campbell, CA 55008
(408) 374-3720

Institute for the Medical
   Humanities
The University of Texas Medical
   Branch
Galveston, TX 77550
(409) 761-2376

Institute of Medicine and
   Humanities
P.O. Box 4587
Missoula, MT 59806
(406) 543-7271

International Bioethics Institute
250 Masonic Avenue
San Francisco, CA 94118
(415) 564-1148

Kennedy Institute of Ethics
Georgetown University
Washington, DC 20057
(202) 687-3885
Library: (800) MED-ETHX

Midwest Bioethics Center
410 Archibald
Suite 106
Kansas City, MO 64111
(816) 756-2713

Northwest Institute of Ethics and
the Life Sciences
5 West Harrison Street
Seattle, WA 98119
(206) 281-0177

Regional Center for the Study of
Bioethics
Medical College of Wisconsin
8701 Watertown Plank Road
Milwaukee, WI 53226
(414) 257-8498

CANADA

Center for Bioethics
Clinical Research Institute of
Montreal
110 Pine Avenue West
Montreal, Quebec, PQ H2W 1R7
Canada
(514) 842-1481

Centre for Professional and Applied
Ethics
University College
University of Manitoba
500 Dysart Road
Winnipeg, Manitoba R3T 2M8
Canada

Groupe de Recherche en
Bioéthique
Université de Montréal
Case Postale 6128, Succursale "A"
Montreal, Quebec H3C 3J7
Canada

Groupe de Recherche en Ethique
Medical
Université Laval
Quebec, Quebec G1K 7P4
Canada

Groupe de Recherche Ethos
Université du Québec à Rimouski
Rimouski, Québec G5L 3A1
Canada

University of Calgary Medical
Ethics Research Program
The University of Calgary
3330 Hospital Drive, NW
Calgary, Alberta T2N 4N1
Canada

Westminster Institute for Ethics
and Human Values
Westminster College
361 Windermere Road
London, Ontario N6G 2K3
Canada

EUROPE, ASIA, AND AUSTRALIA

Bioethics and Environment Society
Regional Research Laboratory
Hoshangabad Road
Bhopal-462 026
India

Centre d'études Bioéthiques
51, Promenade de l'Alma
Bat. 43/45 34B
1200 Brussels
Belgium

Centre for Biomedical Ethics
Development
Jl. Kramat V1/7
Jakarta, Pusat
Indonesia

Centro di Bioetica dell' Università
Cattolica del Sacro Coore
Largo Francesco Vito, 1
Rome, Italy 00167

Comité Consultatif National
D'Ethique pour les Sciences
de la Vie de la Santé
101, rue de Tolbiac
75654 Paris
France

The Dietrich Bonhoeffer
International Institute for
Bioethical Studies
GPO Box 588
Adelaide SA 5001
Australia

Dipartimento di Bio-etica della
Fondazione
Internazionale Fatebenefratelli
Rome, Italy

FIAMC Bio-Medical Ethics Centre
(Federation of Catholic Medical
Associations)
St. Pius X College
Aarey Road, Goregaon East
Bombay 400 063
India

Ian Ramsey Centre
St. Cross College
Oxford OX1 3LZ
England

Institute of Medical Ethics
(Publishers of the IME Bulletin)
151 Great Portland Street
London W1N 5PB
England

Institute of Medical Ethics
Tavistock House North
Tavistock Square
London WC 1H 9LG
England

Institute voor Gezondheids Ethiek
Bonefantenstratt 4
Maastricht
Netherlands

International Institute of Bioethics
P.O. Box 419
L-2014
Luxembourg

Linacre Center for the Study of
Ethics of Health Care
60 Grove End Road
St. John's Wood
London
England

Monash Centre for Human
Bioethics
Monash University
Wellington Road
Clayton, Victoria
Australia 3168

DEATH AND DYING

Americans Against Human
Suffering
2506 Canada Boulevard, #2
P.O. Box 11001
Glendale, CA 91206
(818) 240-1986

Association for Death Education
and Counseling
638 Prospect Avenue
Hartford, CT 06105
(203) 232-4825

Concern for Dying
250 West 57th Street
Suite 831
New York, NY 10117
(212) 246-6962

Hemlock Society
P.O. Box 11830
Eugene, OR 97440
(503) 342-5748

Society for the Right to Die
250 West 57th Street
New York, NY 10107
(212) 246-6973

HEALTH-CARE ECONOMICS AND PUBLIC POLICY

Health Care Financing Administration
6325 Security Boulevard
Baltimore, MD 21207
(301) 966-3000
Oversees the Medicare and Medicaid programs and related federal medical-care quality control staffs.

Health Security Action Council
1757 N Street, NW
Washington, DC 20036
(202) 223-9685
Composed of individuals and organizations that attempt to increase support for national health insurance and progressive health plans through publicity and education.

People's Medical Society
462 Walnut Street
Lower Level
Allentown, PA 18102
(215) 967-2136
Promotes citizen involvement in the cost, quality, and management of the American health-care system.

U.S. Department of Health and Human Services
Inspector General's Hotline
(800) 368-5779
(301) 965-5953
Handles complaints regarding fraud, waste, and abuse of government funds, including Medicare, Medicaid, and Social Security.

MEDICAL RESEARCH AND EXPERIMENTATION

Animals' Agenda
456 Monroe Turnpike
Monroe, CT 06468
(203) 452-0446

Foundation for Biomedical Research
818 Connecticut Avenue, NW
Washington, DC 20006
(202) 457-0654

Physicians' Committee for Responsible Medicine
5100 Wisconsin Avenue, #404
Washington, DC 20016
(202) 686-2210

Public Responsibility in Medicine and Research
132 Boylston Street
Boston, MA 02116
(617) 423-4112

ORGAN AND TISSUE TRANSPLANTATION

American Council on Transplantation
700 North Fairfax Street
Suite 505
Alexandria, VA 22314
(703) 836-4301
(800) ACT-GIVE

The Living Bank
P.O. Box 6725
Houston, Texas 77265
(713) 961-9431
(800) 528-2971

United Network for Organ Sharing
1100 Boulders Parkway
Suite 500
Richmond, VA 23225
(804) 330-8500
(800) 24-DONOR

REPRODUCTION

The American Fertility Society
Suite 201
2131 Magnolia Avenue
Birmingham, AL 35256
(205) 251-9764

Americans United for Life
343 South Dearborn
Suite 1804
Chicago, IL 60604
(312) 786-9494

Choice
c/o Women's Way
125 South Ninth Street
Suite 603
Philadelphia, PA 19107
(215) 592-7644
Reproductive Health Care Hot Line:
(215) 592-0550
Child Care Hot Line:
(215) 592-7616

Human Life International
7845-E Airpark Road
Gaithersburg, MD 20879
(301) 670-7884

National Abortion Federation
900 Pennsylvania Avenue, SE
Washington, DC 20003
(202) 667-5881

Planned Parenthood Federation of
America
810 7th Avenue
New York, NY 10019
(212) 541-7800
Hot Line: (800) 223-3303

FURTHER READING

GENERAL

Chapman, Carleton B. *Physicians, Law and Ethics.* New York: New York University Press, 1984.

Childress, James F., and Ruth D. Gaare, eds. *Biolaw: A Legal Reporter on Medicine, Health Care and Bioengineering.* Frederick, MD: University Publications of America, 1986.

Heintze, Carl. *Medical Ethics.* New York: Watts, 1987.

Inlanders, Charles B., Lowell S. Levin, and Ed Weiner. *Medicine on Trial.* New York: Prentice-Hall, 1988.

Macklin, Ruth. *Mortal Choices: Bioethics in Today's World.* New York: Pantheon Books, 1987.

Malmsheimer, Richard. *"Doctors Only": The Evolving Image of the American Physician.* Westport, CT: Greenwood, 1988.

Melhado, Evan M., Walter Feinberg, and Harold M. Swartz, eds. *Money, Power, and Health Care.* Ann Arbor, MI: Health Administration Press, 1988.

Palmer, Larry I. *Law, Medicine, and Social Justice.* Louisville, KY: Westminister, 1989.

Scully, Thomas, M.D., and Celia Scully. *Playing God: The New World of Medical Choices.* New York: Simon & Schuster, 1987.

Strosberg, Martin A., I. Alan Fein, and James D. Carroll, eds. *Rationing of Medical Care for the Critically Ill.* Washington, DC: Brookings Institution, 1989.

Veatch, Robert M., ed. *Medical Ethics.* Boston: Jones & Bartlett, 1988.

Walters, LeRoy, and Tamar Joy Kahn, eds. *Bibliography of Bioethics.* Vol. 13. Washington, DC: Kennedy Institute of Ethics, 1987.

Young, Ernle. *Alpha and Omega: Ethics at the Frontiers of Life and Death.* Reading, MA: Addison-Wesley, 1989.

DEATH AND DYING

Brody, Jane. "Most States Recognize the Legality of a 'Living Will,' But Few Americans Invoke It." *New York Times*, September 21, 1989.

Downing, A. B., and Barbara Smolen. *Voluntary Euthanasia: Experts Debate the Right to Die*. London, England: Peter Owen Publishers, 1986.

Knox, Jean. *Death and Dying*. New York: Chelsea House, 1989.

Robertson, John A. *The Rights of the Critically Ill*. New York: Bantam Books, 1983.

Society for the Right to Die. *Handbook of Living Will Laws*. New York: Society for the Right to Die, 1987.

U.S. Congress, Office of Technology Assessment. *Institutional Protocols for Decisions About Life Sustaining Treatments*. (OTA-BA-389). Washington, DC: Government Printing Office, 1988.

Weir, Robert F., ed. *Ethical Issues in Death and Dying*. New York: Columbia University Press, 1986.

MEDICAL RESEARCH
AND EXPERIMENTATION

Altman, Lawrence K. *Who Goes First? The Story of Self-Experimentation in Medicine*. New York: Random House, 1987.

Bevan, Nicholas. *AIDS & Drugs*. New York: Watts, 1988.

Check, William A. *AIDS*. New York: Chelsea House, 1988.

Fetal Transplants. "Nightline," with Ted Koppel. (Show no. 1728). ABC News. January 6, 1988.

Hawkes, Nigel. *AIDS*. New York: Watts, 1987.

Hershey, Nathan, and Robert D. Miller. *Human Experimentation and the Law*. Germantown, MD: Aspen Systems Corp., 1976

Jones, James H. *Bad Blood: The Tuskegee Syphilis Experiment*. New York: The Free Press, 1981.

Magel, Charles R. *A Bibliography on Animal Rights & Related Matters*. Lanham, MD: University Press of America, 1981.

U.S. Congress, Office of Technology Assessment. *Medical Testing and Health Insurance*. Washington, DC: Government Printing Office, 1988.

ORGAN AND TISSUE TRANSPLANTS

"Artificial Heart Implants Can Continue." *FDA Consumer*, March 1986, 5–6.

Deveny, Kathleen, and Alan Hall. "Should Profit Drive Artificial Hearts?" *Business Week*, December 10, 1984, 38–39.

Dowie, Mark. *"We Have a Donor": The Bold New World of Organ Transplants*. New York: St. Martin's Press, 1989.

Freese, Arthur S. *The Bionic People Are Here*. New York: McGraw-Hill, 1979.

The Hastings Center. *Ethical, Legal, and Policy Issues Pertaining to Solid Organ Procurement: A Report of the Project on Organ Transplantation*. Hastings-on-Hudson, NY: The Hastings Center, 1985.

Kittredge, Mary. *Organ Transplants*. New York: Chelsea House, 1989.

Leinwald, Gerald. *Transplants: Today's Medical Miracles*. New York: Watts, 1985.

Lord, Louis J., with Joseph Carey. "Man-made Hearts: A Grim Prognosis." *US News and World Report*, August 18, 1986, 8.

Madison, Arnold. *Transplanted & Artificial Body Organs*. New York: Beaufort Books, 1981.

REPRODUCTION

Andrews, Lori B. *Between Strangers: Surrogate Mothers, Expectant Fathers, & Brave New Babies*. New York: Harper & Row, 1989.

Baird, Robert M. *The Ethics of Abortion: Pro-Life vs. Pro-Choice*. Edited by Robert M. Baird and Stuart E. Rosenbaum. Buffalo, NY: Prometheus Books, 1989.

Brody, Baruch A. *Abortion and the Sanctity of Life: A Philosophical View*. Cambridge, MA: MIT Press, 1985.

Edwards, R. G. *Test-Tube Babies*. Edited by J. J. Head. Burlington, NC: Carolina Biological Supply, 1981.

Frank, Diana, and Marta Vogel. *The Baby Makers*. New York: Carroll & Graf, 1988.

Grenard, Philip, with Jack McGowan. "Embryos in Legal Limbo." *McLean's*, July 2, 1984, 44, 46.

Petchesky, Rosalind P. *Abortion and Women's Choice: The State, Sexuality, and Reproductive Freedom.* New York: Longman, 1984.

Sher, Geoffrey, et al. *In Vitro Fertilization: A Personal and Practical Guide to Making the Decision That Could Change Your Life.* New York: McGraw-Hill, 1989.

Singer, Peter. *Making Babies: The New Science and Ethics of Conception.* New York: Scribners, 1985.

U.S. Congress, Office of Technology Assessment. *Infertility: Medical and Social Choices.* (OTA-BA-358). Washington, DC: Government Printing Office, 1988.

GLOSSARY

ABO system the major human blood type system, which depends on the presence or absence of two antigenic factors, A and B

abortion the termination of a pregnancy; may occur naturally as a miscarriage or be induced artificially, especially by a doctor

AIDS acquired immune deficiency syndrome; an acquired defect in the immune system caused by a virus (HIV) and spread by blood or sexual contact; leaves people vulnerable to certain, often fatal, infections and cancers

amniocentesis a test for genetic defects in an unborn child; cannot be performed until the mother is 14 to 16 weeks pregnant

anencephalic failing to develop a higher brain in the womb

antibody one of several types of globular proteins produced by the body to combat bacteria, viruses, or other foreign substances

antigen a bacteria, virus, or other foreign substance that causes the body to form an antibody

artificial insemination artificial introduction of sperm into the cervix

AZT originally called azidothymidine, and later zidovudine; a drug that inhibits the human immunodeficiency virus (HIV) that causes AIDS

blind test experiment in which the subjects are not told whether they are in the control group or the test group

blood types blood groups; categories into which all humans can be separated on the basis of the presence or absence of certain antigenic factors in their blood

cardiac arrest the cessation and total loss of heart function

CAT scanner computerized axial tomography machine; a type of diagnostic X ray used to give a three-dimensional picture of various parts of the body, such as the brain and spinal cord

cerebral palsy impaired muscle control and speech disturbances caused by brain damage usually incurred during or prior to birth

chromosome rodlike structure that contains genes; 46, grouped into 23 pairs, are present in the nucleus of all human cells except sex cells, in which there are 23 unpaired chromosomes

coma state of deep unconsciousness from which a person cannot be roused

control group a comparison group against which a group undergoing an experimental procedure may be evaluated

cryopreservation preservation of biological materials at very low temperatures in order to maintain the viability of those materials for further use; used to preserve human semen for artificial insemination

cyclosporine a drug that helps to prevent rejection of transplanted organs by inhibiting some functions of the body's immune system; approved by the FDA in 1983

defensive medicine medical care that is excessively precautionary and essentially unnecessary

DNA deoxyribonucleic acid; a nucleic acid composed of two strands of nucleotides; the strands are wound around each other in a shape called a double helix and are linked together by hydrogen bonds between the bases of the nucleotides; DNA contains the chemical instructions for determining an organism's inherited characteristics

DNR orders "do-not-resuscitate" orders; orders that provide a basis for the decision as to when patients should and should not be resuscitated

double-blind test experiment in which neither the subjects nor the doctors know which subjects are receiving the test drug or which are receiving the placebo

ethics the branch of philosophy dealing with moral principles or values

eugenics the study of and methods for genetically improving a species

euthanasia mercy killing; the deliberate ending of the life of a person suffering from an incurable or painful disease: passive euthanasia is the termination of life support treatment, thereby resulting in death; active euthanasia involves taking an action, such as giving a lethal injection, to cause death when it would not otherwise occur

experimental medicine the scientific study of disease through research, involving the use of treatments and procedures of unproven effectiveness

FDA Food and Drug Administration; agency of the U.S. Public Health Service that attempts to protect the public from unsafe foods and drugs by enforcing the health and safety laws passed by Congress; its tasks include the extensive testing of new drugs before they are made available to the public and the regulation of the manufacture and sale of approved drugs

freestanding surgical center medical facility that performs surgery but is not associated with a specific hospital

genes complex units of chemical material contained within the chromosomes of cells; variations in the patterns formed by the components of genes are responsible for the differences in inherited traits, such as whether a person has blue or brown eyes

genetic engineering a branch of scientific technology that includes various methods of cutting and splicing genetic material, using enzymes both to cut DNA at specific sequences of nucleotides and to rejoin the strands; sometimes this process is carried out within an individual organism, and sometimes genetic material is transferred from one organism to another

genetics the branch of science that deals with the heredity and variation of organisms

heart pacemaker a device designed to stimulate, by electrical impulses, the contraction of the heart muscle at a normal rate, thereby stabilizing the patient's heartbeat

hemophilia an inherited disease whose sufferers lack adequate quantities of one or two of the factors that enable blood to clot; most hemophiliacs are male

Hippocratic oath an oath that embodies a code of medical ethics and is usually taken by those about to begin medical practice

HIV human immunodeficiency virus; the virus that causes AIDS

HMO health maintenance organization; an association that offers health care to voluntarily enrolled individuals for a fixed price determined in advance and paid in installments

hospice an establishment that attends to the physical and emotional needs of terminally ill patients while allowing death to take its natural course

ICU intensive care unit; medical facility especially designed to meet the needs of critically ill patients

imaging device device for taking internal pictures, such as radiologic and ultrasound pictures

infertility impaired or absent ability to produce offspring; in women, an inability to become pregnant; in men, an inability to fertilize eggs

iron lung Drinker respirator; an apparatus for artificial respiration in which alternations in the air pressure of a metal tank enclosing the patient's body force air in and out of the lungs

IVF in vitro fertilization; also called test-tube fertilization; the combination of sperm and egg in a laboratory dish and the subsequent transfer of the fertilized egg into a woman's uterus

Jarvik device mechanical heart, designed by Dr. Robert Jarvik in 1982; originally intended for permanent use, this device has proven suitable only for temporary heart replacement

kidney dialysis a procedure for removing waste products from the blood, used in cases of kidney failure

living will legally binding document applicable in a case of terminal illness in which an individual gives specific directions regarding his or her own treatment or refusal of treatment

malpractice improper medical care resulting from a doctor's carelessness or ignorance

marker an identifiable element that can be used to distinguish, characterize, track, or trace a cell or other biological element

Medicaid a state-administered medical insurance program for the poor, funded partially by the federal government and partially by the state and supervised by the Department of Health and Human Services

medical indigence inability, due to lack of insurance or money, to cover the cost of one's own health care

Medicare a federal medical-insurance program for retired people who are covered by Social Security; funded by payroll taxes and administered by the Department of Health and Human Services

Parkinson's disease a progressive disease of the central nervous system characterized by tremors and slowed muscle movement, usually found in the elderly

placebo inert substance in the form of medication given to patients in a controlled test, either to determine the effectiveness of another medication or to determine whether an illness has a psychological rather than physical cause

polio poliomyelitis; a contagious viral disease, especially common in children, that attacks the central nervous system and can result in paralysis

pre-embryo an egg that has been fertilized in a laboratory dish

quackery allegedly therapeutic practices or methods that are of no benefit and are sometimes dangerous

quadriplegic person whose arms and legs are paralyzed

respirator a device that provides artificial respiration

resuscitate to restore to life or consciousness one who is apparently dead; entails reactivating the heart and sometimes the lungs

Rh factor antigens present on the membranes of red blood cells

Social Security a tax-funded government program that serves two major functions: providing monthly cash payments to the retired and disabled, and contributing funds to the Medicare program

sperm bank clinic holding cryopreserved sperm

surrogate mother a woman who agrees to become artificially inseminated, carry the fetus to term, and then give the newborn child to a specifically appointed party, relinquishing all legal claims as that child's mother

T cell an immune system cell that helps to regulate antibody production

thalidomide a sedative prescribed to alleviate morning sickness in pregnant women in Europe during the late 1950s and early 1960s; eventually discovered to cause serious birth defects

transfusion the introduction of blood into the bloodstream of a person from whom that blood did not originate

transplant the transfer of tissue or an organ from one area of the body to another or to a different person

xenograft heterograft; a graft of tissue transplanted from one animal species to another

INDEX

PICTURE CREDITS

Jeffrey Finn is the senior Washington editor for *AHA News*, a weekly paper on hospital affairs issued by American Hospital Publishing, Inc. He also reviews books for the health magazine of the *Washington Post*. Finn has a B.A. in English and psychology from the University of Michigan, Ann Arbor, and an M.A. in journalism and public affairs from American University in Washington, D.C.

Eliot L. Marshall is a senior writer for *Science* magazine, the weekly publication of the American Association for the Advancement of Science. He has been employed on the magazine's "News and Comment" staff for 10 years, reporting on environmental health, nuclear energy, and science policy. He has also served as a senior editor at *The New Republic*. Marshall is the author of *Legalization: A Debate* in the Chelsea House ENCYCLOPEDIA OF PSYCHOACTIVE DRUGS, SERIES 2.

Dale C. Garell, M.D., is medical director of California Childrens Services, Department of Health Services, County of Los Angeles. He is also clinical professor in the Department of Pediatrics and Family Medicine at the University of Southern California School of Medicine and Visiting associate clinical professor of maternal and child health at the University of Hawaii School of Public Health. From 1963 to 1974, he was medical director of the Division of Adolescent Medicine at Children's Hospital in Los Angeles. Dr. Garell has served as president of the Society for Adolescent Medicine, chairman of the youth committee of the American Academy of Pediatrics, and as a forum member of the White House Conference on Children (1970) and White House Conference on Youth (1971). He has also been a member of the editorial board of the *American Journal of Diseases of Children*.

C. Everett Koop, M.D., Sc.D., is former Surgeon General, Deputy Assistant Secretary for Health, and Director of the Office of International Health of the U.S. Public Health Service. A pediatric surgeon with an international reputation, he was previously surgeon-in-chief of Children's Hospital of Philadelphia and professor of pediatric surgery and pediatrics at the University of Pennsylvania. Dr. Koop is the author of more than 175 articles and books on the practice of medicine. He has served as surgery editor of the *Journal of Clinical Pediatrics* and editor-in-chief of the *Journal of Pediatric Surgery*, Dr. Koop has received nine honorary degrees and numerous other awards, including the Denis Brown Gold Medal of the British Association of Paediatric Surgeons, the William E. Ladd Gold Medal of the American Academy of Pediatrics, and the Copernicus Medal of the Surgical Society of Poland. He is a Chevalier of the French Legion of Honor and a member of the Royal College of Surgeons, London.